Luck Favors
the Prepared

Nathaniel Barber

Printed in the United States of America

First Printing, 2017

ISBN 978-0-692-87475-2

Take the Stairs Publishing
PO Box 11717
Portland, OR 97211

Cover design, illustrations and layout by Jaclyn Barber
Author photograph by Eric Ellis

www.nathanielbarber.com
Twitter: @Nathaniel_Bbr
Instagram: Nathaniel_Bbr
Facebook: Luck Favors the Prepared
Email; nathanielbarber@nathanielbarber.com
If you still can't reach me, it wasn't meant to be.

This book is dedicated to Jaclyn. I owe you a Coke.

Disclaimer

This is a work of creative nonfiction. Since I've been cursed with an excellent memory, I am confident these stories are an accurate record of events, for better or worse. The "creative" part is for the sake of the story. Many details are swapped around. Some timelines are expanded while others are condensed. Some names are not changed while others have been changed or are not included at all. It should go without saying, dialogue is not verbatim, as I am not in the habit of recording my daily exchanges. I've written scenes and dialogue and events as I can most honestly recall, and I think you will agree they have been displayed here without flattery or glorification.

Stories

Luck Favors the Prepared

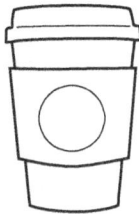

First Impressions

I didn't even want the job.

My interview was out there, on the easternmost edge of Gresham, Oregon. Beyond the turgid clog of Ukrainian strip malls and dollar stores, where even Portland's mighty eastward sprawl concedes its gallop to the opening ranges and foothills of Mt. Hood.

It wasn't much of an interview. More of a get-to-know-you since I'd already been hired for the position.

Commonly defined as a parallel promotion, I was transferring between identical positions from one district nobody wanted anything to do with, to another district, awash with newcomers. This amounted to sliding from one unmoving pool of Store Team Leads and Assistant Store Managers, "STLs" and "ASMs" respectively, to an identically stagnant community of spot-blockers 260-miles to the south. All of us hopelessly dug in to a supervisor caste, tending the unspeakable hope that death or retirement or some other personal tragedy would befall one of the district holdouts, shaking the ranks one position, this way or that.

Even though Portland was more expensive, the job mysteriously paid seventy-five cents less per hour than the one I was leaving.

My new cafe was a drive-through. It was a thirty-five minute commute from my new apartment, along the temperamental Interstate 84. My team would be cordial, for a day or two. But they'd eventually come to believe, as a district implant, I'd stolen their rightful path to middle management. The sole clientele were commuters on their way to work in the morning, coming home at night. In between these two incredibly busy rushes was a long period of desolate inactivity. In spite of this mercurial flow of customers, the store was still burdened by the same excruciating sales quotas as their downtown counterparts.

"Corporate Alchemist" seemed a more fitting title than "Assistant Store Manager."

My interview was during the long midday lull, when nobody actually entered the store. I was met by two suspicious girls at the counter. When I told them who I was, they gave each other a knowing nod.

"I'll get Elise," said one.

It was customary to offer applicants a complimentary beverage for an interview. But both girls went back to chatting in the drive-through window, watching me while I waited for Elise, combing from my old shoes to my new, awful haircut:

"Marine Chic."

Elise was a boisterous, motherly woman with a warm cinnamon roll handshake.

"Were you not offered a beverage?"

I didn't say yes or no.

Rather than bother the girls, Elise made my drink.

The cafe was empty. The retail shelves were fully stocked, faced and smartly curated. Even the packets of sugar at the creamer bar were organized and displayed with an artistic swirl.

"We don't get a lot of walk-ins," she said, handing me a large coffee, black, no room. "Sometimes, there's a lost bicyclist who stops in for water and the bathroom."

Elise gave me the off-script description of the position: in the early hours the line at the drive-through has no end. Every customer is late for work.

"That's what they say," says Elise. "Except, they yell, 'Hurry up! I'm late for work!'"

Then, there's nothing. No customers. The staff spends the hours of nothing cleaning and cleaning and fidgeting until the evening rush, which is another endless line of miserable people after a miserable day of work.

I said, "That sounds awful—"

Elise held up a finger. She said, "There's one more thing."

"What's that?"

She laced her fingers and leaned in, "We're a pretty tight crew here."

"Okay," I said.

"And... we're all women."

She leaned back, letting this sink in. Maybe I was supposed

to be shocked.

This was hardly news.

How many district meetings had I attended where I was the only man in the room? My handicap became especially poignant when discussions occasionally rolled around to our progressive corporate culture of diversity and inclusivity. It was a running joke I'd be asked to contribute something from the "little boy's club."

"Okay?" I said.

"No," she said. "I mean, we're *all* women. Twelve to fifteen employees, depending on the students. But all of us are women."

Again, she gave me a moment to catch my breath.

"Are these zombie women?" I implored. "Or thieving women?"

Elise was shaking her head, like I wasn't understanding something that should have been perfectly obvious.

"Do these women collectively refuse to wash their hands after using the bathroom?"

"No, no," she said. "And good God, no! It's just important… you should know what you're getting yourself into. That's all."

"Alright." I said. "Thank you?"

"Alright then."

She stood and offered me another doughy handshake. As we shook hands, concluding the interview, I noticed the two baristas behind the counter, still watching me. I smiled and gave them a fun little wave, which they ignored. They monitored me as I gathered my papers and saw myself to the door.

When Elise called me that evening, I kindly passed on the job.

She knew that already.

All she had to say was, "Yeah."

I demoted myself to the lowest position in the district, a barista, and secured some throwaway opening shifts in a store downtown. I showed up early for my first day.

It was warm and dry, even at 3:50 in the morning. The sudden raindrops were alarming. No clouds, then more rain, but not rain. I was being showered with piss. From a condo balcony above, someone who turned out to be a regular at my new store chased me with his stream, cackling like a drunk jackass.

This is the moment my new Store Team Lead saw me from across the street, burning obscenities at the balcony above. He approached cautiously, holding out his hand.

"No!" I said. "No. I'm soaked in piss!"

The Landlord

I should start here, after the divorce, when I became a landlord.

I've always loathed landlords. Every one of them the same: aloof, greedy and cruel. Doubly so for those overseeing properties in our college town. They raised rent with impunity and cared little about the breathtaking tales of unjust evictions and horror stories of broken furnaces, missing windows and persistent leaks.

If I had to be a landlord, I would be a good landlord. My rental would shine as an example of how an entire market could be run: attentively, with generosity and fairness.

I set the rent low, covering only my own monthly mortgage plus fifty dollars to cover the time I would spend managing the property. I refused to deal with a property management company because they would only charge me a fortune to turn my beautiful tenants into a profit margin, similarly ignoring their pleas for maintenance, repairs and improvements. I, on the other hand, would personally attend to my tenants' needs, promptly and completely. The people who rented my home would have a happy, affordable home. They would tell all their friends about their wonderful rental. Their friends, in turn, would rise up, demanding similar treatment.

My little rental was the seed that would change the world.

That is how stupid I was.

A whole week passed after posting my world-changing rental, and I received only one response.

Tina Messenger's first emails were friendly and generously sprinkled with catchphrases like "family in need" and "low income" and "looking for a happy, safe home in the beautiful Pacific Northwest." All of which played right into my idiotic scheme.

Tina's husband, Jim-Bob, took a job at Shell's Puget Sound oil refinery. They were moving from the suburbs of Dallas–Fort Worth, Texas with their three children, in search of a better life.

She confided she was unsure this was the right decision. Moving to a different city, she was apprehensive about the relocation.

"But is it nice?" she wrote. *"Is Bellingham a nice place? Is it a good place for children? Is there a lot of stuff to do, like outdoors?"*

I said it was. I enjoyed it very much. Like her, I too was moving to a new city and was very sad to leave. As for children, I didn't have any, but I saw many children in and around the area. They all seemed to be doing okay, happy even. So I told her that.

She wrote back, *"What about the school district for this neighborhood? What have you heard about it? Is it good?"*

I said I could not vouch for the school district, but I rode by many of the schools on a daily basis and they looked, at least from the street, to be in good repair. With no broken windows and attractive playgrounds.

"How about restaurants?" she wanted to know. *"Is there a mall close by? And grocery stores? Isn't it always raining?"*

I dutifully answered all her questions.

From all these unimportant details relayed in our obnoxious correspondence, Tina gleaned the most important detail of all: anyone who'd promptly respond to that many unimportant questions was clearly desperate.

It was quite clever, actually.

After her discovery, when our discussion led inevitably to the nuts and bolts of the lease, all her aw-shucks charm suddenly evaporated.

"I can assure you," she wrote. *"An in-person interview is not possible at all."*

She explained why a humdrum vetting for prospective tenants was not only impossible for her, but excessive and placed undue financial strain on her family.

"Remember," she reminded. *"We live so far away, in the suburbs of Dallas–Fort Worth, Texas. We're not some oil rich Texans off Dallas. I AM A COWGIRL, and proud of it!!!! And a MOM. We live MODESTLY, from PAYCHECK to PAYCHECK so you can't just DEMAND we come all the way up there just so you can*

have your in-person interview. You've got my references. I gave you so many references!!! That will have to do. And we'll need to know by tomorrow. This evening would be better since I got to let the movers know for sure."

Her messages raised many alarms, but these were effectively silenced by my own rapidly approaching departure. My two new jobs in Portland began the first of the next month, less than two weeks away.

I could certainly not afford to let my house sit vacant for a whole month.

Her emails grew increasingly erratic. In my panic, I passed off her dependence on the caps-lock key and excessive exclamation points as some backwards Texan quirk. Like referring to herself as a "cowgirl" when she and her roughneck husband live in the suburbs of Dallas–Fort Worth.

At least she did have many references, which I methodically grilled with pointed, probing questions.

Did the Messengers consistently pay their rent in full? On time? Did they provide the first and last month's rent and a security deposit? On time? What was the condition of the house when they left? Were they good tenants? Surprise pets? Outrageous demands? Would you rent to them again? Hmmmmm?

Wouldn't you know it? The contacts at several rental agencies, even neighbors and former employers answered every question in the affirmative. It's as if the whole state of Texas was desperately in love with the Messengers, gushing syrupy southern praise at the very mention of their name. They all agreed, unequivocally, that Tina and her husband and even her three kids were the salt of the earth. Model tenants.

It was an effervescent endorsement, sparkling with the same enthusiasm only a used car salesman could drum up for a Fourth of July tent-sale. The kind that's easy to misinterpret for good news.

While I had suspicions, they seemed unfounded since it would indicate the entire state of Texas had pulled together an unprecedented groundswell to dispose of the Messengers.

Our rental agreement was finally signed. It was a one-year lease.

As soon as the paperwork was completed Tina gave me a new phone number to use if I needed to get ahold of her. It was for a pager. *"If you need to contact me,"* she wrote, *"you may use the PAGER ONLY!!!!! If you attempt to contact me directly, I will consider it a VIOLATION of my rights as a renter."*

I called the number.

There was a click and a long pause. A shrill metallic school-marm took the line, commanding me to type my phone number. I typed in my phone number and when I put the phone to my ear, the line was dead. Thinking I'd somehow hung up, I called again. Again, the tiny demon requested my phone number, which I did.

Moments later, Tina called.

"What?!"

"I'm sorry, what?"

"What do you want?! You paged me *twice*?!"

"I wanted to test the pager. I didn't know people still used them."

"Why would I give you a pager number if people didn't use pagers? I use a pager!"

"I got that." I said. "Why can I not call you directly?"

"*You have no right* to call me directly!"

"Tina," I said. "I didn't have any plans to contact you directly but—"

"Yet, you paged me. Twice."

"But what if I need to get ahold of—"

"Here I am just slipping into the bath. My very first moment alone in WEEKS! When all of a sudden my damn pager is blowing up!"

"Tina," I said, in my best Mr. Rogers. "Some time in the next year I may need to get ahold of you."

"Then use the fucking pager!"

Again, the line went dead.

Somewhere in the suburbs of Dallas–Fort Worth, Tina locked herself in the bathroom, away from her husband and her kids, with a scattering of vanilla candles, a box of moscato and Shania Twain.

She slid into a lavish bubblebath, cursing my name.

Tina would prove not only incapable of receiving phone calls, but impossible with even the most banal transactions.

When it came to paying her rent, she couldn't just send in a plain old rent check. She insisted on paying her rent with a Western Union money order that cost twelve dollars to send and took four business days to clear. Often, when those four days happened to straddle a weekend the check wouldn't clear for six whole days. Or worse yet, the seven or eight days it would take to traverse a holiday weekend.

Whole empires have risen and fallen in half the time it took to clear a check from Tina Messenger.

When her first rent check arrived, it was twelve dollars short. Tina had made sure to extract Western Union's processing fee from her monthly total and, while she insisted her payment was on time, her check wouldn't clear until four days after my mortgage was due.

I didn't bother paging.

In a diplomatic, friendly email, I suggested these terms were preposterous.

Tina responded flatly, *"Bring it up with Western Union."* She continued, *"Also, I will not be paying the deposit for security or last month's rent without having seen the rental. It is not FAIR to request I pay any extra money for a rental sight-unseen."*

It was both weird and appropriate when my ex-wife knocked on the front door to her own home. The door was, after all, half hers.

Of course, I let her in. We stood in the entry, smiled and emptily asked after each other. We shook hands and got to the work of sorting our furniture and the final clean-up for the Messengers.

She was maybe surprised to hear I'd been able to rent the house. Maybe even impressed. Naturally, she had many questions about the family who'd be at the helm of our sole investment for the upcoming year. If I had made any impression on my ex-wife for establishing and managing a rental property, it didn't take long for it to vanish since my answers only seemed to inspire a myriad of additional questions, and panic.

While our marriage had been a difficult marriage, at least our separation and divorce was civil and businesslike. That did not mean, however, I was in any mood to answer her many questions or, for that matter, attempt to calm her down.

"You haven't even met them?!"

She was starting to yell.

"No," I said. "It's a long story."

"I guess! You got a first and last month's rent? Right? A twenty percent security deposit?"

"It's complicated."

"What?!"

"Listen," I said. "Just butt out and take your DVDs."

Historically, such a rebuttal would lead to another of our wicked, protracted brawls. All that was behind us now, thank God. We just kind of let it go, resigning to opposite ends of the house to sort, to clean up our mess.

The last thing my ex-wife told me was to take care of the cats. This was a reasonable request. Especially since I'd been so adamant about taking them. They might have been our cats, but really, they were *my* cats. All three of them and they'd been worked into a perfect lather by the last nineteen-hour marathon of cleaning and packing. Maybe they could sense the terrible journey ahead.

Their worst fears were confirmed as they were lured into a carrier and added to the van. They howled and wailed in unison.

I completed this last, long trip with earplugs.

They were still screaming, five hours later, as I parked the van outside the Presidential Court Apartments just as the residents, my new neighbors, were leaving for work that morning. They sized me up suspiciously as I unloaded my satanic cat choir and hurried them up to our new home—the tiny studio apartment we'd all be sharing for the next year. The cats stopped yowling soon as I released them into their new habitat.

It only took a moment for them to paw around the perimeter and back to me.

"Nice closet," they meowed. "Where's the rest?"

Meanwhile, out on the street, a parking officer was sharking around my van with his notebook. He assured me I was not allowed to park and unload my things.

"You should've got someone to help you move," he said. "At least someone to stay with the van while you unload."

I agreed, that would have been nice.

I asked, "Would you like to be that special someone?"

He answered, "…no."

I promised to be quick. I told him about the broken elevator and the three flights of stairs and how there wasn't any parking for blocks.

He shrugged and said, "Take it up with city council."

He gave my rental van a kick in the tire, took out his pamphlet of citations, "Who should I make this out to?"

The closest parking spot was four blocks away but hard won after a half hour of slinking my van around Northwest Portland like a child predator.

It was four blocks to the Presidential Court, with all I could capture in my tiny arms, three flights of stairs to deposit the pile in the apartment, back downstairs and four blocks to the van. I completed this journey many, many times. A microwave full of books, a queen-sized mattress, a drumset and boxes brimming with books and dishes and condiments and clothes and shoes and shit until my new living room, the only room in the studio, resembled a Humboldt County yard sale.

I'd given myself plenty of time, but now there were only twenty minutes left to return downstairs, sprint the four blocks and drop off the rental van (without a delay) and arrive, on time, to my first day at my new job after twenty-four hours of violent exercise.

When I arrived for new employee orientation at the Oregon Museum of Science and Industry, I was pouring sweat and heaving for air, happily shaking everyone's hand like a coked-up jackass while, outside at the bike racks, someone was using a battery-powered angle grinder to saw through my bike lock.

I hadn't even thought to bring a lunch.

Somewhere in this blur, Tina and her family passed overhead on the Marquam bridge. They were only hours away from their new home.

It had been a horrible trip for the Messenger family. Far worse than mine since, from the moment they pulled out of their Dallas–Fort Worth driveway, everything had gone terribly wrong.

I would soon hear all about it, as if I'd been the sadistic travel agent who'd tricked them into this wringer.

"You *said*," said Tina. "The trip would only take three days!"

"No," I said. "I *said* it could be done, easily, in three days."

"Yeah, but you didn't tell me Disneyland would be right next to I-5! Have you ever driven past Disneyland with a car full of kids?! You never told me a day at Disneyland with three kids with the 'fastpass'... that, and every hotel between Texas and here would eat up the last of our savings."

"Oh yeah," she continued. "That's another thing. We maxed out the last credit card just to get here. So you can kiss that security deposit, that last month's rent goodbye. You'll be lucky if we can even pay next month's rent at all!"

I guessed she hadn't noticed the impeccable state of the house. The spotless floors and dust-free windowsills. Not to mention, the lone mint I'd left on the kitchen counter.

They weren't even in the entry, with all their bags, when that husband of hers went straight to work on the hot water heater.

When he found the device, it was in working condition and looking forward to many years of happy service. But he was convinced it wasn't heating water hot enough.

From Tina's report—

"He didn't even TOUCH the thing!!!! All's he did was turn a couple knobs and tightened a bolt or two when all of a sudden, all of the connections just CRUMBLED into CRUMBS!!!! As I write this message I AM STANDING IN AN INCH OF WATER THAT IS COVERING THE ENTIRE DOWNSTAIRS!!!!!"

"You need to make this right. IMMEDIATELY!!!!!" She caps-locked. *"What are you going to do about this?!"*

She followed this email with a rambling of complaints:

"I was looking forward to one of the famously LUSH, FULL Pacific Northwest lawns I've heard so much about. Your lawn has

so many bald patches! What's your plan of action here?"

And

"Some of the windows don't open, and some that open, only open half way. Why didn't you tell me about the window malfunctions? When can we expect a repair man?"

And

"Have you ever looked into getting the house insulated? It is INCREDIBLY drafty, my husband had to turn on the stove on high so we could keep from FREEZING through the night, in addition to running the heater at FULL BLAST!!!!! I'm worried the only way to address this problem is with some serious remodeling and you can't expect us to pay your full rent if we're living in a house that's under heavy construction!"

And

"I think you need a new roof."

And

"PLEASE PLEASE PLEASE," she concluded. *"PLEASE let me know what time tomorrow we can expect the new water heater?!!!!"*

I bought a new water heater on a credit card. I'd never done such a thing before, and the swagger of this careless purchase was a little intoxicating. I even hired a plumber to install the appliance, also on the credit card. I was really on a roll.

While the heater wasn't the Cadillac Tina had picked out, she was kind enough to let it pass. Everything was all set for the next day.

That next day turned out to be the busiest day the museum had ever seen. All records for daily attendance were broken as we were hosting the new *Body Worlds* exhibit. It attracted hordes of people from all over America.

By some mystifying twist, the owners of *Body Worlds* had stipulated in their contract with the museum there would be no exchanges or refunds for tickets. Not for any reason. Under no circumstances, at all, absolutely, positively *no one* would be allowed to change the time of their ticket or receive a refund. For any reason. Whatsoever.

As the new guy, I was given the unfortunate job to handle refunds and exchanges, which is to say, it was my unlucky charge to refuse either option.

While the exhibit itself was certainly incredible, perhaps its most interesting, if unintended, phenomena was the spectrum of colorful reactions it inspired at the front desk. Most notably, what happens when an American is faced with a hard and final "NO" to either an exchange or refund. I was, on numerous occasions, personally threatened with ruinous legal revenge.

Little did I know, how soon I would become intimately familiar with leveled threats of belligerent civil lawsuits.

That's when I got a call from the plumber.

I was being chewed out by a sunburned Floridian named Chauncy wearing a Corona visor. I couldn't look away from his red and scabby scalp. He was raising all sorts of hell about how he and his wife and his kids schlepped themselves over three hundred miles of hot coals to see this exhibit but arrived a day after their scheduled viewing. I put my phone on silent just as another call was rolling in, this time from Tina. Then another call, and another.

I finally wrapped things up with Chauncy, who promised

me our "discussion" was only beginning. I hadn't seen the last of him, oh no. And when he was through with me—

I checked the first message from the toilet: "Hey there! This is Don. The plumber. I'm here with your water heater. I'm standing on your porch aaaaand I'm ready to go. But the tenant won't let me inside. Actually, she's refusing to even open the door. Please give me a call aaaas soon as possible."

Tina had also left messages, which at first sounded like a bad connection chopped up the recording. Another listen revealed there was nothing wrong with the recording. It was Tina. She was furious, that much was clear. The rest however, was word salad. A horrible regurgitation of vowels and crying and yelps. There were some consonants in there too, but mostly it was just animal sounds.

I sent Tina a page.

We were so short staffed, there at the front desk, that when Tina finally called me back, there was nobody to take my place. I simply left, putting up a little sign that said, "Be right back!" with a smiley face.

The next person, who'd spent their tenure in line formulating the most brutal opening gawked, stuttering, at my little sign.

"Ohhh no!" he shouted. "NO! No no non onononon no—" and was still swearing at me when I stepped out to answer the phone.

Tina was in hysterics, "What's your fucking problem Nate?! HUH?!!"

"I just got a call from the hot water guy. What is going—"

"Yeah, he's out there, standing on your—*my* porch, and

he's trying to break into our house!" She hissed, "He tried the knob!"

"It's okay, Tina. He's there to replace the water heater!"

"No, it's not okay! That is *not okay*. The Washington State Residential Landlord/Tenant Act states that if a landlord or an employee of the landlord wants to gain access to a residence they are required, *by law*, to provide the tenants with forty-eight hours notice."

"I C.C.'d you on the confirmation with the hot water guy."

"Last night!"

"And I paged!"

"Yeah, so you couldn't even have the balls to tell me in person?"

I didn't have an answer for that last one. I was being watched. The long line of ticket holders were waiting for me to return. They might as well have come to the zoo, watching me through the glass, yelling at my phone.

"*But you got the message?*"

"Yes! I got your stupid message. That's not the point! That was last night. Here we are, it's morning and the Washington State Residential Landlord/Tenant Act clearly states—" she stopped. She was yelling off the phone, presumably at the hot water guy on my porch, "Stop knocking you goddamned psychopath! You'll have to come back tomorrow!"

This, he obliged her. Don, the plumber, left and promptly added a seventy-five dollar charge to his bill for the inconvenience.

Tina took to email.

"*I want you to know, if you were hoping me and my family wouldn't notice we have to go an extra day without hot water then you are SORELY MISTAKEN!!!"*

I was curious, how would Tina exact her revenge?

The next day, the plumber exchanged the hot water heater in a flash. He reported what he saw, how the house was deserted. How the living room and the kitchen were like a rat nest but he was in and out of there without one word to the lady of the house.

When I didn't hear from Tina for the remainder of the month, I was convinced a bullet had been dodged. Until the deadline for rent came and went.

None of my pages were answered.

Finally, Tina wrote in an email, *"Just so you know, this first month we've suffered in your home, we've been TRICKED to live in INTOLERABLE conditions!!! I and my husband will have to get back to you about how much we'll be taking out of this next month's rent for this hot water thing, and the THOUSANDS of other HORRIBLE INCONVENIENCES we've had to put up with!!!!"*

It is worth noting, when she sent this email, her rent was already two days late. It was November 2, 2007. Why do I remember this? All these many years later?

November 2 was a Friday. The Messengers, like Western Union, didn't "do" weekends, so it was unlikely they'd reveal their verdict until the following Monday, but they certainly wouldn't be paying (if at all) until Tuesday, which meant, knowing Western Union, there'd be a tiny window between when the money was released that following Friday and when they'd close for the weekend. But probably not. Then I'd have to wait until the following Monday, the twelfth, for the money to clear so I could escort the still-warm cash to the bank across the street where my mortgage was almost two weeks late.

It is also worth noting, the high that came from dumping a brand new hot water heater and its ungodly installation fee all on a credit card was still zesty in the autumn air. So this is when, in a straight panic, I paid the month's mortgage on the same credit card. While this effectively maxed out the limit, the shot of relief that followed this profoundly idiotic move was simply divine.

"Finally," her email concluded. *"I want you to know I'm sending a copy of this email to my lawyers."*

The Washington State Residential Landlord/Tenant Act is as narcotic a read as its title suggests. It could only be interesting to insomniacs and Tina Messenger. God bless her, she managed to take this chalky pith of legalese and wring it like a sponge full of cash. I'd only performed a cursory skim of the document in my scant preparations to become World's Greatest Landlord. In truth, I understood very little about its complexities and was interested in its minutiae even less.

I was satisfied to glean the broad strokes: Washington State tenants were rightly fortified with a robust list of protections and clearly defined provisions for conflict resolution and filing and meeting complaints. Essential human rights.

As a renter of numerous apartments and homes it would have served me well to have been better acquainted with the Revised Code of Washington index as Tina had clearly been. After her several overtures to the document I decided to give it another look.

I poured over the RCW, eager to find the chapter which out-lined how renters were within their rights to open a porthole of suck in your home.

I was unable to locate this chapter.

What I did find was the good work of the Northwest Justice Project and the Tenants Union of Washington State. Both organizations had done an excellent job to boil down and serve up the RCW as bite-sized morsels, translated into digest-ible English.

It was here I discovered an eviction could actually take three weeks or even more to carry out. I also learned if I served Tina a three-day Pay or Vacate notice, somehow orchestrat-ing the simultaneous delivery of two copies: one by mail, one hand delivered or pinned to her door (trickier than it sounds), she could simply ignore it. There'd be nothing more to say in the matter until I ponied-up for a lawyer and filed an unlawful detainer lawsuit. While this would be the only legal method of shucking the Messengers from my beloved home, it also prom-ised to be a lengthiest and most costly.

Further down the rabbit hole, I found that even if I won this costly legal battle, Tina could still refuse to budge, at which point I would have to file the court findings with the local sheriff and hire the local sheriff and a number of deputies to pry them loose. Again, for a healthy fee.

Littered throughout this path of nauseous research were several links to legal resources and law offices for tenants in trouble, who needed to discuss their particular issue with a real, live human being.

I followed one of these links and was put in touch with a

sympathetic secretary at the Tenants Union of Washington State who provided the number for a law firm expert in representing even the shadiest dispute.

This is how I fell madly in love with Rory.

Rory was a paralegal and coffee jockey for So & So Law and Associates. He was not a lawyer, per se. He only assisted the lawyers who represented tenants. Because of this, I assume, he was not bound by the same restrictive language a lawyer was so keen to employ.

"Start from the beginning, Trevor," he said, calling me by the fake name I gave him. "Tell me all about this joker."

I could hear him wagging back and forth in his chair, smacking spearmint gum.

For Rory, I put on my best Tina.

I caught him up to date on the last eight months: how I'd been lured from Texas to our dream home, only to discover we'd been tricked into a cesspool of nightmare. How, shortly after settling in, I lost my job at the oil refinery (just as Jim-Bob had) and couldn't get another job because I suffered from chronic back pain and my wife can't work because she had three children to raise and me to take care of. This meant we were physically incapable of an income.

That "physically incapable" part, I wished I could take credit for that. That phrase, and this whole windy sob story was plagiarized from Tina's emails and phone calls.

"Okaaaay," said Rory. "Physically...innnncaaaapable..." He was taking notes as I rattled on about how we've been forced to live in squalid conditions (one of Tina's favorite

27

catchphrases) since our arrival.

"Whoa whoa whoa," said Rory. "Squalid like how? Unsafe? Infestation? Toxic? Repairs he's ignored?"

Again I referred to Tina's notes and recited her litany of complaints. The house was drafty and cold, everything was dark, the floors creaked too much, there were bald patches in the yard, the toilets didn't flush right and there wasn't enough water pressure and the trees dropped too many pine needles. The driveway needed to be repaved. Insulation, roofing, electrical, plumbing, foundation and landscaping all needed to be completely redone.

"So this is why I've been shorting my monthly rent."

"What's that?!" said Rory with a little cough. "Repeat that last part?"

"Well," I said, quoting Tina. "I can't be expected to live in these conditions! Every month, my wife and I add up the things we've had trouble with to deduct them from our monthly rent."

"Have you...sent these deductions to your landlord?"

"Yes."

"How?"

"Email, mostly. Other months I just call him up to give him a list in case he's interested in why the rent's short."

"Anything with a signature? Your signature?"

"Naw," I said. "Just email and talking on the phone."

"Okay...talking onnnn...the, phone," Rory said, taking this all down. "Good, good. Nothing in writing. Well, it's not *good*. But it's not terrible. Very difficult to submit this as actual evidence in a small claims court. The receipts for your money orders, on the other hand..."

"You mean, my landlord could take us to court?"

"Well," said Rory. "If you do get hauled into court, you may be able to diminish the landlord's chances of victory. Perhaps you can point to shoddy paperwork in the preparation of the eviction lawsuit. Or maybe the landlord's illegal behavior, such as not maintaining the rental property in a habitable condition which, as you described, is wide open to interpretation. All this will serve as a good defense, as would a claim that the eviction lawsuit is in retaliation for your insistence on needed, major repairs."

I scribbled all this down frantically.

"Also tricky," continued Rory. "Subtitle II in Housing Code 22.206.160, Section C...hold on, I've got it here...okay that part's called 'Just Cause for Eviction: The tenant habitually fails to pay rent when due which causes the owner to notify the tenant, *in writing*, of late rent four or more times in a twelve-month period."

"Shit," I said. "That's totally us. We've paid rent on time twice, out of eight months."

"Did your landlord submit a written delinquency notice in the mail and hand deliver an identical copy?"

"Nope," I said, chomping down on my knuckles. "Just calling or email."

"Then you're good to go! Listen, Trevor, the guy you're renting from, this is just his own home, right? He's not rich, and he probably doesn't know any lawyers so he's not going to be keen to file a summons and complaint against you. They can be very costly. He's not like, a man who nets multiple properties and he's not associated with any rental agency? What I mean to say is, he doesn't have a lot of clout."

Rory continued, "He's a guppy."

"Let's say," I said. "Hypothetically, I just stop paying rent. What then?"

I could hear him creaking back in his chair, kicking his feet up. I guessed he's had so many "hypothetical" conversations with deadbeat tenants, he was genuinely grateful to be having a frank discussion about screwing it to the landlord.

"Well," said Rory. "That's more a question of philosophy than renter's policy. But I suppose, to answer your question directly, your situation, if you're going to carry out what you described, which I cannot officially condone, it would not, in the larger sense, improve relationships between tenants and landlords in Washington State."

He waited.

"Further," he finally continued. "On a larger scale, I guess over time, this could make things difficult for others. Single mothers, say. Or victims of domestic abuse and refugees. People who are experiencing real problems—"

"BUT THAT'S US!" I yelled, channeling my inner Tina. "That's us! *We* have real problems. So how can I keep from being evicted?"

"Well, that's easy, Trevor." he chucked. "Pay your rent. In full and on time. And be good tenants...why—are you laughing?"

After hemorrhaging cash for months, I'd taken a third job at a bakery to fill any remaining hours I wasn't already working. While I was finally able to make progress paying down the credit card, I was seldom at home.

By all appearances, I'd moved to Portland for the sole purpose of work.

The time I spent at home, three hours at night and two hours in the afternoon, I slept. Or, I tried to sleep.

Downstairs, two floors below and one unit to the south, one of my neighbors (all our studio windows opened to the same dreary courtyard) had recently taken to learning the drums.

While she took up her new instrument with enthusiasm, her playing indicated little interest for the beats and rhythm of which the instrument was capable. She focused more on the sounds the individual pieces could produce. As such, her playing was erratic and disjointed. The occasional cymbal crash and snare roll. Thirty seconds of silence then a thundering rumble of the toms and kick drum.

Our community of the Presidential Court apartments had grown accustomed to what sounded like an occasional gunshot but was just a random whack at a snare drum.

The few hours I had to catch up on sleep were spent imagining my neighbor tooling around her apartment. She'd get up for a bowl of cereal, notice the drumset and decide to give that kick drum two minutes of what-for and shake the Presidential Court like a JELL-O mold.

One of these delirious nights, I was half awake and panicking. I think I sent Tina a three-day Pay or Vacate notice, but I couldn't be sure. According to my notes, I had. But had I done everything correctly? The Tenants Act seemed more concerned with how the notices were delivered than their actual content. There was a receipt for the courier I hired to post the notice on her door (nobody would answer the doorbell, of course) timed to deliver within hours of an identical copy arriving in her mail.

This was confirmed by Tina's reply which, sadly, did not include a rent check. Instead it was a letter from a fake lawyer.

The fake lawyer wanted me to know the property was in such disrepair, that I'd ignored so many requests for improvements and because I'd tricked them into moving into a hellhole, she would pay her rent when she was good and ready. Less, of course, what she and her husband considered were the appropriate deductions.

Of course.

Of course, I answered her letter with a letter from a real lawyer. I paid him handsomely too. He whipped up an official something-or-other notifying her she could pay the rent or tangle with an eviction lawsuit.

Her reply was a rent check, paid in full and suspiciously absent of commentary.

This was a thoughtful gesture, but since it arrived two weeks late, I responded with a second late payment notice. This she answered with another letter stating she had grounds to sue me for discrimination, citing the Fair Housing Act, 42 USC s. 3601 et.seq. A 1988 state law, which, among other things, recognizes protection to individuals for marital status, physical disability and familial status (having children). Whatever that means.

My response, and the only letter my lawyer happily prepared pro bono, summarized in fantastically dry legalese the following sentiment: bullshit.

Our correspondence had become a nauseating volley of one-upmanship by way of the US mail.

By the close of the tenth month, my lawyer sent a final notice: I was breaking the lease! This was two months early but, I wrote, everyone concerned could not disagree: this had been an awful experiment. The Messengers had proven my lofty mission to save the world, one affordable home at a time, was laughable folly.

"You're throwing us out?! Into the COLD?!?!?!" she wrote. *"It isn't FAIR. IT ISN'T RIGHT! What do you expect us to do now?!?!?! I hope you know we'll be right here for your next tenants. We'll be right here to answer any of their questions about what it was like renting from* you. *Because of this, I EXTREMELY suggest you reconsider—"*

She went on and on.

The short version: she planned to throw every last of her abundant legal resources in my path, and when the sheriff came to pry her fingers from my banister, she promised that's all that would be left, a banister and a smoldering pit.

I was reminded of Chauncy, the sunburned Floridian, and his promise of a ruinous civil lawsuit for refusing to refund his *Body Worlds* tickets. By then I still hadn't heard from Chauncy or his lawyers. It was doubtful I ever would.

Somewhere in the mix, Tina overlooked a three-day Pay or Vacate notice my lawyer sent by mail and courier. I guess we'd thrown so much at the Messengers, something finally stuck, and when it lapsed, (thank God) I put the house on the market.

The appraisal, the showing and the inspection were all accomplished with the Messengers spitting threats at their visitors like a den of snakes. In spite of this, the house sold in under a week. I took a three-day weekend to return to my home to clean up after the Messengers and prepare for the new owners.

I knocked on my own front door.

Nothing.

I opened the door. I said, "HellooOOooo?"

The Messengers had evaporated from the property. All that remained was a two-liter bottle of Faygo, spinning on the greasy kitchen floor.

The layer of grease was so thick I had to hold out my arms to balance across the kitchen. An oily sheen covered the cupboards and windows and countertops: proof it hadn't all been a dream.

I never actually met the Messengers so I couldn't say for sure any of this had actually occurred. Maybe it was all some horrible fever dream, punctured by the seizure of drumbeats downstairs.

Somebody had been living here. Somebody with a yen for fried food.

I spent the weekend cleaning and repairing my beautiful home. I unleashed an arsenal of industrial chemicals thick with fumes, even as my huge box fan (lovingly nicknamed "The Sheriff") chopped up and evicted the air, thick as a deep-fried fart, outside.

I could describe my last walk-through. The house, my house, after it was clean. Every room empty. The curtains pulled. That much I'll keep for just me.

That part is mine.

Band Geek

Mr. Millson

Skeeter ran around our hotel telling everyone the news. When he finally found Ian and me, he was breathless and doubled over, heaving for air.

"You'll never—omygod I can't breathe! Whew! Guess what happened!"

"What?!" I said.

"Fucking Mrs. Millson is what—just caught Fucking Mr. Millson fucking one of the first chair flutists in her hotel room!"

"Whoa!" I said. "Which one?!"

"Seriously? Who do you think? Betty Bertelstein."

Of course.

Betty was Mr. Millson's eyes and ears in the music department. She sat across from me in band. Even as a junior, she was a hard-ass. Vaguely fundamental, either Jehovah's Witness or Mormon, she dressed exclusively in shapeless dresses and pantsuits. When she wasn't playing her flute she maintained a perfect resting position, which, for Betty Bertelstein, was only a slight variation on a constant: ramrod straight, shoulder blades touching in the back with a chin-lock focus on Mr. Millson.

That they were caught together, doing who knows what, only confirmed what everyone had long suspected.

Imagine that. An entire music department swirling with rumors for who knows how long (I was just a freshman) and how few of us were shocked. How acclimated we'd become to Mr. Millson's music department.

Mr. Millson was a short, puggish man. He was skinny except for a cantaloupe gut he not only ignored but allowed to lend heft to his wagging swagger. He was short and compensated for this with a simmering, constant temper, always fired up and red-faced. Even when he was just trying to schmooze an extra scoop of Jell-O from the lunch lady. His lips were not lips, but the absence of lips. Sweaty flaps, really. Fleshy bits of face he pursed to a thin, kissy embouchure under a bulbous, alcoholic nose.

He played hot trumpet. As trumpet players go, he was a swingin' dick. He frequently indulged in unsolicited, lengthy ramblings about the trials and glory of a decades-long career in contemporary jazz, tossing off first-name references like, "When Maynard and I were packing Jazz Alley..." or "That's an interesting question. You know, Miles once told his drummer..."

But here he was, teaching high school band.

It was no secret he was a committed drunk. One of the marching band cymbalists once noted how Mr. Millson only drank coffee early in the morning but was rarely seen without his mug.

Far worse than his fizzing, drunken tantrums was his undying love for sizzling hot jazz.

Jazz-fusion. Free funk. Jazz funk. All the worst genres jazz had coughed up found a loving home in Mr. Millson's first string band, The B-Sharps.

In The B-Sharps, trumpeters and trombonists were charged with the razzle-dazzle, dolling up various pieces, in spite of any composer's intentions. Their syncopated jerks and stabs were contrasted by the saxophone section, which was encouraged to swoop and sway in great, exaggerated scoops, their instruments ungainly as an albatross.

What crowd pleasers!

Even the untouchably cool ballads like "The Girl from Ipanema" or "My Funny Valentine" were gussied up with cartoonishly gimmicked drum solos cut by molten wails and swells from the trumpets.

He conducted a variety of bands, from jazz to classical, but all were marked by one signature feature: a flute section fully stocked with pretty, attentive Betty Bertelsteins who he openly groomed with a predator's shameless persistence.

How this man was able, with so much as a hinty flirt, to render his flutists to overcooked linguini and his trombonists insane with jealousy would remain one of the great unsolved mysteries of Hillcreek Valley High School.

Betty Bertelstein and Mr. Millson had sat together for the entire five-hour bus ride to our hotel in Vancouver, Canada. It was an arrangement that, even after the scandal, would turn out to be identical to the bus ride home.

They'd pawed at each other constantly, loud enough to treat everyone in the bus to every detail of their creepy courtship. Mrs. Millson sat one seat behind them, saying nothing. She looked out the window, her hands folded in her lap.

"They're in there now!" said Skeeter.

"Who?"

"Oh gawd, Barber." He snapped his fingers. "Pay attention!"

"Oh, yeah. Wait, *they're still in her room?*"

"C'mon!"

We ran to the hotel courtyard. The courtyard was an enclosed space the multiple floors of our rooms opened to. There was a hot tub and a fake lawn with fake plants and sunchairs for relaxing. A crowd had gathered around the hot tub in the middle.

"Are they out yet?" I asked.

"Shhh!" they hissed.

It was faint, but there was muffled shouting. It was coming from one of the rooms.

Some of the hardline Millsonites worked feverishly to disperse the crowd.

"You guys," said Tracy the baritone saxophonist. "This is none of our business."

"Yeah!" said Trevor the trombonist. "Leave them alone."

Then a door flew open, two floors up. Mrs. Millson didn't look down to us, just charged straight to the lobby to book a separate room. Eventually Mr. Millson sauntered out, no hint of humility to his same syrupy strut. He set his tummy on the balustrade, looked down at the crowd, which was almost his entire music department. We were agape.

He pointed at us, "No running by the pool!" He shouted, shaking his fist. "You dang kids!"

Everyone thought this was terribly funny. Just like nothing had happened, we went back to playing around the hotel. Betty Bertelstein practiced scales in her room for the remainder of the night.

I was only a freshman then, so I was not yet aware how difficult it would prove to fire a man such as Mr. Millson. Of course, eventually, he was fired. It was rumored his departure was decorated with a generous severance package and a lavish, if sparsely attended, staff luncheon. This was years later, when he finally crossed the line for gross misconduct. Not misconduct with students, of which he was a belligerent, but with ill-gotten district funds. I suppose things were going so well for him, there in his music department, he didn't see anything wrong with spending close to a million taxpayer dollars to build a recording studio in his band room.

In the meantime, however, he was an award-winning band leader. The PTA and the district loved him. He'd built our music department into the envy of the Pacific Northwest. We were regular festival favorites, winning first place in almost every competition and, even though our football team had two perfect seasons of losses, his marching band packed the bleachers for every game.

That's not to say we would escape repercussions for Mr. Millson's indiscretions. It certainly wasn't announced, but a new, mysterious policy was set: any band under his leadership was no longer allowed to participate in events that required an overnight stay. The reasoning for this change was left to speculation. There were vague referrals to budget woes, though it was commonly understood we were spoiled rotten by one of Washington State's most heavily funded music programs.

The day after Mr. Millson was caught with Betty Bertelstein, the event officials were made aware of the situation, and it looked like we'd be heading home early. We'd have to forfeit our spot in the competition finals, and, for that matter, participating in the fully catered awards ceremony. If anyone hated him for it, he certainly didn't let on.

As the event officials considered our fate, Mr. Millson kept up appearances around the hotel, towing the usual entourage, his core, most faithful students. Currently, he was accompanied by Greg, the photographer for our school newspaper: *The Eagle's Nest*. Tracy the baritone saxophonist and Dave, the Dungeons and Dragons drummer. They followed him around the courtyard, from one group of kids to another. He cracked unfunny jokes. Pointed out various made-up stains on people's shirts then flicked their noses, whether they looked down or not.

I watched this sorry procession from the hotel cafe, where I was privately enjoying a soft-serve vanilla ice-cream cone.

When the group stopped by the cafe for a snack, Mr. Millson spied me from the counter.

"Well," he crowed. "Look at what we have here!"

It was his routine to make an individual impression on every student. Size them up. I was still early in my freshman year and we had not yet had our man-to-man. It became clear, as he saddled that cantaloupe to the empty seat at my table, this was as good a time as any.

He pulled a chair around backwards and plopped down, crossing his arms on the back rest, his entourage attending close by.

"Whatcha eatin'?" said Mr. Millson.

"An ice cream cone," I said.

He pulled it toward him, "You mind if I...have a bite?"

Before I could say no, he brought it to my face, tapping a little dollop of ice cream on the end of my nose.

"Oop!" he said, laughing with Greg, Tracy and Dave. "You got a little something on your face."

So—I'd played music since elementary school. I enjoyed playing music too.

Like anyone who wanted to play music in our school I had, until now, navigated Mr. Millson's labyrinthine gauntlet without drawing much attention. My ultimate goal, of course, was a seat in The B-Sharps.

I desperately wanted to be in that band.

What happened next would secure my seat in the group of castoffs and rejects who populated our unnamed second-string jazz band for the next four years. Even in the theater department across the hall, where Mr. Millson managed to cast himself as default music director, even though it was a whole other department, he would manage to seek me out and ensure that, in whatever capacity I was occupied, it would be a living hell.

Mr. Millson and his groupies were in fawning hysterics over the little ice-cream hat on my nose. They just laughed and laughed. I took the opportunity to put the ice cream in Mr. Millson's face. I smashed all of it, right down to the cone, over his big, dumbass nose.

Everyone stopped laughing. When I got up to leave he just sat there, his jazz hands frozen, blinking through a vaudevillian cream-pie.

After our ill-fated trip, things ramped up from their normal pace in the music department. Mr. Millson, perhaps invigorated by his first place victory at the festival (the officials eventually allowed our bands to play in the finals), combined with his egregiously lenient punishment, now ran the music department with abandon. Betty Bertelstein had a hell of a time cleaning up after him. She soured into even more of a righteous hardass. She started throwing around commands and mock punishments to underlings.

She even snapped at me for running in the hallway.

"Stoppit!" she demanded. "That's dangerous. Someone could get hurt."

Maybe I, too, was feeling a little more brave, after crushing my ice-cream cone in Mr. Millson's face. Even though she outranked me as a junior and Mr. Millson's minion, I suggested instead, she sit on her flute and fuck right off.

She snapped a confirming nod to say, "That's all I needed," turned on a heel and marched straight into Mr. Millson's office. There was faint shouting coming from behind his closed door.

Later that same day, Mr. Millson found me taking apart my

clarinet, "Alright Barber, what's this I hear about you running in the hallway?"

I tried explaining as he frowned into his empty mug. His expression: *this mug sure could use a refill.*

I was a problem for him.

He didn't know what he was going to do with me.

"We got a real problem here," he said. "I don't know what I'm going to do with you, Barber."

Clearly, he was referring to my disregard for Betty Bertelstein. Not the running in the hallway.

He figured out what to do with me soon enough. The next day in our wind ensemble, we were in the middle of a Tchaikovsky piece when, as if he'd just remembered, he tapped his tiny baton on a metal music stand until the band was quiet.

"No, no, no...I'm sorry, class," he said. "This just, is not working. Nate, I need you to pick up your things and go sit on Danny's left."

Betty Bertelstein, effervescent with joy, seemed fit to split her floor-length denim skirt as I was being demoted from first-chair to third-chair clarinet. Last-chair clarinet, actually.

"Go on," he said, pointing at Danny with his baton.

I stood and gathered my things. Danny and the whole clarinet section also had to stand, gather their things and shuffle one seat to fill the recent vacancy. This they dutifully did, though grumbling and complaining, even if it meant they were being promoted. The hushed commentary through the band indicated Mr. Millson had broken an unspoken rule. Such adjustments were only executed after biannual tryouts and posted on a new seating chart, prepared and distributed by Betty Bertelstein.

If Betty was upset by this disruption in protocol, you'd never notice. She beamed and beamed at this display of swift chivalry on her behalf. I thought she would stand and applaud.

After I settled into my new seat, Danny Bedwell leaned in and said, "Don't worry, man. Mr. Millson is a penis."

Danny, it turned out, was a nice enough guy. Even if he was just learning how to play his instrument. It wasn't long until he quit and, by default, I moved up a chair.

A promotion!

Of course, Danny made the smart move. As did many others, rather than endure open ridicule. By midyear, Mr. Millson had whittled the group down to a tight-knit band of ruthless devotees. And me, of course.

Why didn't I quit? Maybe I was too childish, or just curious to see what would happen with four years, strapped into last-chair clarinet. As it happened, I would find out during our Winter Formal Concert: a black-and-white tuxedo affair the winter of my senior year.

Volunteers

I used to play B-flat clarinet in wind ensemble, but I switched to contrabass clarinet for political reasons. Since there were only two of us, the contrabass section could remain unaffili-ated but still friendly with the big party bosses of Mr. Millson's band. Eventually, I learned to enjoy playing contrabass clari-net, even if it was like wrapping my lips around the tailpipe of a 1957 Buick.

I played alto saxophone in the nameless, second jazz band,

but I switched to baritone saxophone because that got me as far away from the soprano saxophonist as spatially possible. Not that I didn't like Tracy Trimble. She was not the issue. It was that horrible instrument of hers. Soprano saxophones are, hands down, the worst instruments ever created. The child molester of the woodwind section.

I also played baritone saxophone in marching band. I had a complete marching band outfit with spats, shoulder epaulettes and a breast piece that spelled out "EAGLES." Our hats were tall, furry and deep red. Undoubtedly it was the hats that inspired our band's nickname: The Lockstep Tampons.

While I enjoyed playing music in various bands, Mr. Millson and many of my classmates offered frequent reminders of how I had no business being there. Which was okay.

Their suggestion was, while I could play my instruments just fine, my attitude presented a mockery of everyone who preferred to take band dead seriously.

Band.

Seriously. How could anybody think high school band was so important? My lousy attitude was maybe the only point on which Mr. Millson, his core elite and I could agree.

Music was supposed to be fun! If not fun, then at least funny. It was hard work, yes. But anyone who bothered to take even a fleeting glance at the baritone saxophone's part on "Born to be Wild" or "Jungle Fever" knew it would not impress any college admissions board.

Or worse, parents.

Worse yet, friends.

Sometimes, students would run crying out of Mr. Millson's band room. Some came back, others did not. The stress! It was enough to break even the most confident goody-goodies down to pudding. They would be found crumpled in the band department hallway, or locked away in one of the practice rooms, their muffled sobs bounding down the echoing corridor.

A bassoonist was sent into throes after a telltale squeak spoiled her audition.

What a wuss!

Sometimes, however, Mr. Millson intentionally broke his students, and that was ugly. This was never pretty to watch. Even when it was someone you wanted to burn.

This is how it happened.

Mr. Millson would stop the music, whatever we were playing. He'd determined something was not right. He'd sniff out the culprit and ask them to stand.

It was not a request.

We'd wait until they stood.

Together, they'd take it from the top. Mr. Millson conducting his prey, until the eventual mistake. There was always a mistake. Narrow that troubled riff to the surrounding measures and this Mr. Millson had them repeat, and repeat, and repeat for him and the for whole class.

"Again," he'd say. Arms crossed, facing not them, or even the band. Maybe something on the floor, a piece of dust he soccered with the toe of his polished wing-tips as the measures were recited again and again.

"Again."

He'd pace, hands on hips, watching the floor.

"Again."

Once he even went to his office to shuffle some papers.

"Again," he shouted from his office. Throwing the papers.

"Again! Again! Again!"

Once, he even broke a mug.

Of course, he never bothered explaining what should be played differently, what change should be made. It was implied. It was supposed to be obvious, which made the poor student who couldn't glean the error all the more stupid.

"Again!"

On and on like this, until the student was successfully broken. It was a simple procedure.

Of course, I had my turn as well. I was so excited. My part was quite fun to play, actually. Even if standing to play a '57 Buick was not so comfortable. I just kept wheeling through my part like a gleeful nincompoop. By the time the bell rang, Mr. Millson was digging his fingernails into his scalp.

"No, no, no, no, no! Barber!" he said, banging with his baton. "Again!"

"But I have lunch."

"Until it's right. Again!"

"But there's lunch," I said, disassembling the Buick. "I am…going to…go now."

I would not get off so easily.

Class was dismissed, everyone rushed for the door except Theresa Aylee, captain for woodwinds. She was shouldering upstream through the push of students, their ungainly

47

instruments and sheet music. She was coming for me.

Every section had unofficial captains. The woodwinds had Theresa Aylee and Betty Bertelstein. The brass had Tyler Henshaw and Steve Dill. They were always eagerly standing by to pick up where Mr. Millson left off.

"Maybe," said Theresa, "We can go over your part after school?"

"I'm sorry," I said. "I work after school."

"Or, we can go through that trouble spot again, during lunch? We could do it together!"

"Because that's a substitute for lunch?" I asked. "Thank you. No."

Skeeter, the snare drummer, had warned me about this. He'd prepared me with a helpful hint: never accept your captain's offer for private lessons. Never, ever.

"Don't you want to get better?" she stammered.

"Of course I do!" I said.

"Then what do you propose?"

"Are you serious?"

"Look, Barber," she looked at her feet, a Millson mimic. "I know—we all know, you don't give a shit about band—"

"That's not true!" I said. "I care."

She was skeptical.

Theresa was rarely seen out of her letterman's jacket. Like a career army general, her breast was a mess of badges and pins. Several pieces of flair representing a prize or commendation for each extracurricular activity, of which she was a key participant.

Putting away my Buick, I couldn't help but stare at those

medals and pins and patches. It all seemed so terribly pathetic. So sad. Still it was she who was telling me the least I could do.

"The least you could do," she continued. "Is sign up to make some money."

"What's that?" I asked. She had my attention.

"I'm glad you asked!" she said. "Follow me."

Theresa pointed out the volunteer board. It was a sign-up sheet posted on the band-hall bulletin board. I'd seen it, of course, but never investigated it because of the word "volunteer."

She explained how it worked.

There were a number of activities you could do to make money. Each of them paid five dollars an hour. There was a car wash next Sunday (5 hours). Or I could contribute baked goods or cashier for a bake sale at various basketball games (2.5 hours or 50¢ per baked item sold).

Further down was a posting for "UW Concessions (8 hours)."

"What's this one?" I asked.

"Do you like football?"

"Do I look like I like football?"

"It doesn't matter. You won't get to see the game anyway. It helps if you like football."

The shift was five hours in a concession stand with an hour-and-a-half set up and clean up on either end. This was at the famous University of Washington football stadium, the Dawg House.

"So I could work eight hours?"

"Sure!"

"And make forty dollars?"

"You bet!"

"I get to keep."

"In your band account, yes."

It turned out, we all had band accounts. Even I had one. Who knew?

Theresa pointed to my name, one of the many next to a big "$0." The high earners were at the top of the list. They were who you'd expect. Some of them had almost four hundred dollars in their account!

"Yes," said Theresa. "It's quite a competition."

She pointed out her own name. "I'm doing okay at $275, but I can do better. I've got half the year to get up to four hundred dollars. You're just a sophomore, so you have lots of time to get there."

"Right on," I said. "When do we get to take this money out?"

"For band trips," she said. "I mean, if you want to spend the money on yourself. Which is fine, but, this music department is in such desperate need—"

"So I can't take the money out? I can't spend it?"

"Ha ha!" she laughed.

I was not trying to be funny.

"Of course not! Silly. We mostly donate ours to the department. Or, if you really want to, you can use it on band trips. Those cost money after all. But if you use funds for trips, then you drop in the ranks, see?"

She pointed out that Jason Miller, the trumpet player, just used one hundred and twenty dollars to help pay for our recent trips to Tacoma, Everett and Marysville. That brought his account to a pitiful sixty dollars. Consequently, his name dropped from the top fifteen to almost the bottom of the list.

He was just above all the zeros, barely.

Jason was a junior, so there was still time for him to get his numbers up there before graduating next year.

"Wait," I said. "Why would you want to graduate with money in your account? Then you can't use it."

"No. But you win the contest."

"What contest?"

"The contest to see who graduates with the most money in their account! Jeez. Silly."

Theresa gave me time to let this sink in.

"That," I told Theresa. "Is probably the stupidest thing I have ever heard. Sign me up."

What did volunteering to work a college football concessions have to do with making me a better musician? It was anybody's guess.

Skeeter suggested a connection, "Why does the Karate Kid wax Mr. Miyagi's car?"

"So he can become a better musician?"

"Precisely."

It would remain a mystery.

One thing was certain, Theresa immediately reported the news to Mr. Millson. Mr. Millson came out of his office to shake my hand. He even went out of his way to make a joke, commenting when I took my seat in the next rehearsal for wind ensemble.

"Heyyy, there he is!" with his jazz hands. "Watch out! This cat's deadly with a vanilla ice cream cone."

There was nervous laughter.

I was on my way!

We started early on a Saturday morning. I carpooled with Skeeter and his sisters and we arrived hours before kick-off. The parking lot for the Dawg House was massive and empty. The only other people there were the first hardcore tailgaters. They were grilling meat. They sounded drunk, which, at that hour, was either "already drunk" or "still drunk."

"Is that steak?" said someone. "Seriously, I think those assholes are grilling steak."

One of the band-moms, Steve Dill's mom Geena, pulled up in her gigantic van. Eighty-four kids burst out to run around the parking lot and throw rocks at each other.

We'd caught the tailgaters' attention. Like *we* were the ones causing a scene.

She brought our paperwork, signed us in for our shifts and gave each of us a t-shirt. Printed on the front: "Follow me! I'm marching in HVHS Marching Band!"

"You can't be serious," I told Skeeter.

"Steak or hot dogs," said someone else. "Who eats steak and hot dogs at six in the morning?"

Skeeter had already wrapped the bottom of his shirt up into his collar and posed with his hands behind his head.

"Oh boys," he groaned at the tailgaters. "Come get your... hawt dawgs."

"That's not funny!" scolded Geena. "This is serious! We're

here to provide customer service, but most of all, you are here as the face of *Hillcreek Valley High School Marching Band.* Show a little school pride."

The nuts and bolts were easy enough to grasp. We each had a register of two hundred dollars and plenty of change. We were shown how to start the hot dog bath.

The hot dog bath was an aluminum cauldron. It was filled then heated to hot dog water temperature. A wire grid down the middle separated the regular ball park franks on one side— those were called plain old "hot dogs." Their larger counterpart, the Polish wieners, were put on the other side. These were called the "Husky Dawg" after the University's mascot.

There was no way to put the hot dogs and the Husky Dawgs in the cauldron without splashing the hot, greasy water everywhere.

Everything else was a piece of cake. Soda pop, candy and don't let the popcorn get low. By eight o'clock the doors opened and we were instantly swamped by a crowd fifteen-people deep.

Pandemonium.

The cauldron was working overtime trying to keep the hot dog water up to temperature, not that it mattered any, since the moment a handful of frozen dogs were dropped into the bath, they became indistinguishable from the hot dogs that were hot and safe to eat.

The floor was instantly awash in hot dog grease. This made fetching a soda troublesome, especially at my register, furthest from the fountain. That meant slipping all the way to the other end of the concession stand to fill the soda order, then sliming all the way back without dropping anything. Eventually I discovered, with a hard shove off the opposite counter and stiff legs, it was possible to slide the entire length of floor and, with some accuracy, land within inches of your desired soda spigot.

Back and forth we went! A disgusting, but efficient, game of hot dog shuffleboard.

We were in it now: the big time.

For halftime, we were relieved from our posts by the band-moms. We joined the remainder of our marching band, which was waiting for us on the Huskies end zone. Mr. Millson was steaming up and down the ranks, inspecting everyone's uniforms.

He was in his full pre-game strut, gripping his hands behind his back. Bits of foam worked into beads where the edges of his lips, if he had lips, would be.

He barked at a trombonist to remember his steps, "We don't want a repeat of the last time, do we?"

We all shook our head. Nobody wanted a repeat of the last time, even if no one knew what that meant.

Mr. Millson reminded Tammy the piccoloist, and for anyone else who may have forgotten, of our last parade when she got nervous and threw up. He asked her if she was going to throw up again.

She looked like she was going to be sick.

"You see this?" he yelled, wedging a toe into the ground. "Astroturf. No puking. Unless you want to come out after halftime and vacuum it up?"

She swallowed hard, gagged and swallowed and gagged again.

An announcer boomed over the stadium speakers, "Ladies and gentlemen! Won't you please give a warm Huskies welcome to Mr. Millson and the *Hillcreek Valley Eagles Marching Band.*"

Mr. Millson barked, "Hup!" and we stormed the field, a great flood of bounding tampons in full tilt. I worried my shoes, soaked through with hot dog water, would attract the attention of the UW mascot, a real husky named Kodiak, prancing at the sideline, fluffy and attentive.

I took my place on the 45-yard line. Thankfully, downwind from Kodiak. I was somewhere in a great letter "H."

Mr. Millson took his time getting to the conductor's platform. He was remarkably comfortable with making an entire stadium of people wait as he sauntered over, his hands in his pocket. He stopped, shook the hand of the Huskies band leader, who was standing by to lend us his field.

We posed still and held our breath for Mr. Millson to take the platform. What was taking him so long?

I got my first look at the stands. They were packed solid. It seemed there wasn't an empty seat in all of the Dawg House, and all of them had come out today not to watch football, but to see me play.

I was famous!

"Hey, Barber," a bass drummer spat close to my shoe. "Check it out."

He pointed with his mallet at Mr. Millson, who was standing on the podium smiling into the sun. He just stood there, soaking up the crowd.

To capture the moment, the bass drummer titled this little vignette: "A pig in shit."

A stab from a whistle snapped us into order. The baton…

A boy, about my age, and his dad came through my line at the concession stand.

He was reading my shirt, "Follow me! I'm marching in HVHS Marching Band!"

"Were you in the Eagles marching band? Down there on the field?"

"Yes," I said. I was so proud. "We're the Eagles."

"Pigeons, is more like it," said the boy. "Y'all sounded like dogshit. And you can't march for crap."

His father said nothing, just mechanically recited a gigantic order from the menu above my head. I took his cash, but the boy stood straight at me, leaning his hands on my counter. I looked down, counting their change, but he pressed in, smiling.

"Hey, guy—" he said. I shoved off the counter. He watched as I sailed by the other registers to the soda machine.

When I returned with their pop, the boy repeated, "Did you hear me? What I said? Y'all look like a bunch of tampons runnin' with your string on fire. Y'all look like—"

"Hey. Jerkoff." Skeeter chimed in from the register next to me. "*We serve your food.*"

That's when Mr. Millson suddenly appeared, between Skeeter and me.

He hadn't forgotten to drop by the concession stand. He was either ego-drunk from his ride on the conductor's platform, or he was just plain alcohol-drunk. He'd definitely heard what Skeeter said but threw a buddy-arm around us both.

To the boy in my line he said, "Are these jokers giving you

a hard time?"

Actually, the boy said nothing. He seemed stunned to encounter this figure, even more pathetic than I was.

Thank you, Mr. Millson!

"Here go—" said Mr. Millson. He dropped a box of Goobers on the counter with a wink. "On the house."

There it went: the last trace of novelty there was to working a stadium concession stand departed with that complimentary box of Goobers.

There were still two hours left.

My second day at the concession stand I started taking twenty-minute bathroom breaks.

There I was, hiding in a bathroom stall, feeling sorry for myself. It was a beautiful day! Not a cloud in the sky. Sure, I could steal a glimpse of the game, here and there, none of which made any sense. Surely, the day was ruined. I was marinated in hot dog grease, my shoes were destroyed, my arms were caked with popcorn salt...

Just then, as I was calculating my misfortune, someone jumped into the stall next to me and slammed the door shut. There was hurried fumbling next door. A pair of bright white tennis shoes, dancing in place.

"Oh geez!" said a deep, heavy voice. The sound of a belt buckle clanging around. "Oh geez! Oh geez!"

The white tennies—dancing, dancing.

Then, when the pants dropped, he either tripped or lost his balance. He seemed drunk. Whatever the reason, the man lunged forward, catching himself against the door of the stall, crapping everywhere.

He crapped all over his pants, and on the floor and on his pants and bright white tennies again. It was horrifying.

"Oh my god!" shouted the man in the stall opposite those skidding, shat-on tennies. "Oh my god! Gross, dude. Gross!"

I moved my feet and legs away from the opening to avoid any splatter. Thankfully, I had only come to the bathroom to hide out, so I pulled up and left in a jiffy. Though not without washing my hands. Twice.

A crowd of grown men, frantic with their belts, pushed for the door.

This was the early nineties, mind you. No cell phones or texting. His car, if he drove one, was somewhere, out there, in that massive parking lot. An ocean of cars. What then? He'd have to walk out there, presumably squishing around in those same pants. Even then, he'd have to sit in his own driver's seat, unless there was a bag or blanket to carry him for the journey home. Or someplace safe.

It had not occurred to me, or anybody else, to notify security to give him a hand. We just ran. He was on his own.

I walked back to our concession stand, impressed, by how totally screwed that guy was.

I thought I was having a bad day!

"Nate Barber: $80."

There it was. Proof.

If I still didn't belong in band, maybe I could buy my way in. Even if I was among the lowest earners.

Theresa, still in that oversized letterman's jacket, caught

me looking up my name.

"Congratulations," she said. "It's addicting isn't it?"

"How's that?"

"The rush," she said, not trying to be funny. "The thrill of getting in there, being a part of the band."

I said I didn't know.

"Well, you know, last Saturday there was another game. We missed you there, at the concession stand."

I said, "Okay."

"You were such a help the last time," she took the cap off a ballpoint pen and located the upcoming date for the next concession shift. "You want me to sign you up for the next one?"

"Oh, no no," I said. "Thank you though."

"You mean, you won't work at the concession stand?"

"Thank you," I repeated. "Not ever. Never again."

"You know," she said, looking left and right and coming in close. She wanted to tell me a secret. "The next game is the Apple Cup." She said this behind her cupped hand, in case there were others listening in. She didn't want to cause a riot.

"What's that?"

"The Apple Cup?! Huskies versus Cougars. It's a wild rivalry. It's gonna be slammin'!"

"So, busier?"

"Way busier. Like, twice as busy. It's going to be awesome!"

"Do I get paid more?"

Theresa came back down from the clouds. "Paid more?" She blinked, six times. "Of course not."

"So I'll work twice as hard for the same money? Money I can't spend at the Seven-Eleven?"

"But you—"

"Pass," I said. "I'll pass."

And dang if she didn't turn and huff directly into Mr. Millson's office.

Winter Formal Concert

The end of summer, the last hot weeks before my senior year began, I met my new counselor, Maurine Clark. She shook my hand and said, "I'm Maurine Clark, your new counselor. If I look like a drowned rat, it's because I hate summer."

I fell in love with her instantly. Which was helpful, because she was about to tell me some very bad news.

I asked, "What happened to Traci?"

"I think she got fired. Or she quit. Anyway, she's not here anymore."

Traci had been my counselor since I was a freshman. Sure, she might've been a little simple, but she never protested when, every trimester, I'd enrolled in jazz band, wind ensemble, theater and choir. Like me, she was not fond of the required courses. She only seemed interested in the progress of our band department. She adored the gossip and goings-on. She even called Mr. Millson a "cutie" which made me shudder.

Our sessions passed quickly as Traci easily lost track of time blissfully reminising her own days in band. She wished, more than anything, she could go back and do it all over again.

It was not easy, a partnership such as ours. But if it meant I would graduate on four years of fluff, I was willing to sit through just about anything, except algebra.

I wondered, before Traci left, had she notified Miss Clark of our tacit agreement?

Things seemed to be going well, until Miss Clark opened my transcripts and gave them a good look. She put a hand on her mouth, concealing either nausea or shock. Or both. She read on, eventually coming up for air.

"You're, uh…a senior?" she asked.

"Of course!" I said.

She started again, at the beginning of my transcripts. Maybe there was something she missed? She made it all the way through my paperwork with the same dour expression. She calmly reset her glasses and laid her hand on the folder, for want of a beginning.

"Do you know," she said slowly, as you would to a nincompoop. "What an *elective* is?"

"Sure!" I said.

"Good," she said. "That's good."

She turned and clacked something into her computer.

"It appears that you are very fond of music."

"I like music. Yes."

"And theater."

I shrugged. "It's okay, I guess."

"But not so much, the required courses?"

"I don't know."

"Yes…well," she said. "I've looked through your transcripts. A number of times now, and I am sorry, but I have some very bad news."

"Oh?" I said.

When Maurine suggested I enroll in CLIP, I was nonplussed. I'd always assumed CLIP was a nicer way of saying "special education."

"Isn't CLIP for retards?"

She looked out the window and sighed.

"Kids are still using that word then?"

"What word?"

"Never mind." She took off her glasses and rubbed the bridge of her nose. "In some cases, yes."

CLIP, it turned out, stood for "contracted learning for an individual pace." She said, some people may not thrive in a traditional classroom setting. In other cases they just want out of school as soon as possible. All the requirements are there. The material is all there. It's just completed in a packet instead of a classroom.

"Okay." I said.

"Okay, good?"

"Yes. Good."

"Good, because without CLIP, you should know, you won't graduate for another year and a half."

"Sign me up."

We walked together to the CLIP office where two teachers were busy getting their room set up for the new year.

"Bethany and Laura," said Maurine. "I'd like you to meet your first recruit. He'll need to complete these to graduate… this year." She gave me a solid clap on my back. She said, "Bon voyage!"

She left me with Bethany and Laura and my list of courses. They looked over my files, surprised by its contents.

"I'd like to start right away," I said.

"I guess so," said Bethany.

They gave me five courses, to begin. Before handing over the packets, they had to be graded.

"What grades do you want?" asked Laura.

"'A's would be nice."

"If you turn in anything that grades below an A, it's a fail. Are you sure?"

I nodded.

"Do the work," suggested Bethany. "Do it right. And God willing, do it quickly. We'll see about getting you out of here in time for graduation."

Laura followed up, "No promises."

I chowed through so many courses in four months, I became a sort of default liaison for the department. Contracted packet learning was still very much a fledgling concept and our classroom was always being invaded by curious parents, suspicious representatives from other schools and the district board. Bethany and Laura made sure to introduce me to anyone who came by for a tour.

One day, Bethany came by to let me in on a secret, "That group has a pool running. I thought you should know."

"What?"

"On your chances for graduation. They're coming by to inspect your odds."

"I know you're joking—"

"Am I?"

She crossed her arms, eyebrows raised.

"How are the odds?" I was genuinely curious.

Bethany demurred, "Four months in, you've managed some impressive results. But I'd say your odds have progressed from 'highly unrealistic,' to 'very highly unrealistic.'"

"That doesn't sound good."

"It doesn't, does it?"

We stayed there, looking over my piles of homework spread on the table.

"There is one thing you can do. And I'm sure you know where I'm going with this."

"I do not."

Of course I knew where this was headed.

"Band," she said. "Kick it to the curb."

Band rehearsals were becoming nearly intolerable. This was typical of the weeks leading to any important concert. Mr Millson was plagued by the same notion—everything was coming unravelled.

He often interrupted rehearsals, not because anything was really wrong, but just so he could wax poetic about the indelible stain failure or incompetence could leave on both his professional reputation and our own academic careers.

He made it clear he was not above revenge, if threats inspired excellence. He assured his students anyone who'd consider us for college would certainly come around, asking him for reference. Except he didn't say "reference."

What he actually said was "blessing."

"What then?" he asked. He was genuinely curious. "Am I to *lie* about how poorly you performed in band?"

This had its desired effect, since being denied entry to college meant no career or marriage, or family or car or home and on and on. The downward spiral that began in the Hillcreek Valley music department ended in a lonely and anonymous death, our two-week-old corpse discovered in a ditch.

It was hard to watch a grown man succumb to the whimsy of his own pathological vanity, armed with no practical means, or desire for that matter, to reign in its compounding spasms of hysteria. What's worse was so many of his students, my class-mates, were susceptible to this morbid lapse in perspective and fell in with his horrible charade. Theirs was a panic that spread like blood in water, poisoning the ranks until even the most cynical of us were stricken by a mysterious fear of failure.

For wind ensemble, the months of increasing pressure finally snapped when Mr. Millson forgot his words during the last rehearsal before the pinnacle event of our musical year: the Winter Formal Concert.

From what we could piece together, the world had finally turned against him. All of his students had either completely forgotten their parts or there was a mutiny and we refused to play anything correctly. Whatever the case, he broke a baton on his stand and now it was his turn to storm out of the classroom. Before he disappeared he regained his faculties to the extent that his words, for better or worse, had returned to him.

"I am marching," he foamed. "Straight to the vice-princi-pal's office. And do you know what I am going to tell Mr. Allen?"

He waited for one of us to guess. Nobody took a swing.

It was a mystery.

"Fuck it!" he said, throwing his hands. "The whole thing!

I'm cancelling the Winter Formal Concert."

He threw open the door and stormed out. He was heard, halfway down the band department hallway, *"What are you looking at?!"*

Free day! We were free to go. Until next period at least. But nobody left.

We obediently stayed put, aside for the flute section who dissolved to tears and exaggerated, glucking sobs from various hiding places, Mr. Millson's office or the instrument storage room. Behind me was another sound. A trombonist busy making himself a martyr. His bellyaching went on and on. He was guilty of some supposed mistake. A failure that he wanted everyone to hear about. How he'd let everyone, especially Mr. Millson, down.

It was, as displays of chivalry go, both grotesque and obscene. The suggestion that *he* was the cause of Mr. Millson's generously restrained tantrum and he deserved to be humiliated for it.

Here is what he sounded like:

"I'm an idiot!" he cursed. "Idiot! How many times? Pianissimo at the al coda!" He furiously scribbled a note into his sheet music. "Stupid! Stupid! Pee-an-iss-im-ooooh! Stupid."

Others chimed in, "Hey buddy, we all make mistakes."

And "Don't beat yourself up."

And "Better luck next time."

While this was fun to watch, I couldn't take any more. My head was going to pop.

"You know," I said. "I didn't hear you play anything

wrong."

The trombonist looked at me with icy disgust.

"Oh yeah?" he said. Then followed with the familiar suggestion, "Why don't you shut the fuck up?"

I shrugged, "Have it your way. But it doesn't explain why Mr. Millson is such a raging psychopath."

This, of course, was an overstep which earned a chorus of protests and insults from several directions. I was already getting up to spend the rest of class enjoying a cigarette in the forest beyond the parking lot.

As I was getting up Mr. Millson returned, accompanied by the vice-principal, Mr. Allen. Mr. Millson was sputtering with rabies, still twitching and nervously licking his lips, or where, if he had lips, his lips would be.

Mr. Allen, tall, calm, with hands the size of outfielder's mitts, steadied Mr. Millson by the shoulders then approached the conductor's podium as one would tiptoe through a minefield.

"We will not be cancelling the Winter Formal Concert," he said, holding out those massive hands. At his feet, the spread of sheet music, the broken baton on the floor. "We've all been under a lot of pressure. There are some pretty high tensions running, but we are going to start from the top. We're going to take it cool and easy. Mr. Millson? Girls, will you please take your seats? Girls!"

The sniffling flutists returned from their various hiding places with puffy, raw eyes.

"Mr. Millson," said Mr. Allen. "Please!"

Mr. Millson reluctantly shucked from the wall. Mr. Allen handed him a new baton and surrendered the podium.

Psychopath Millson raised his baton, "From the top... again."

After school, with Bethany's advice still rattling around my head, I stopped by the theater to get a sneak peek at the decorations for our concert that evening. There were some teachers and a small team of students working furiously to transform the empty stage into a twinkling winter wonderland.

It was quite a picture.

Hanging from the ceiling, over the seats and stage were huge, glittery snowflakes. The stage itself was both spare and elegant with tall, white birch branches propped to resemble trees. They were strung with white Christmas lights and glass icicles. A lone cardinal perched on a branch high and left, close enough to the sightline that it was easily overlooked. Puffs of fake snow were strung here and there with a pinecone or sprig of holly.

The whole picture was framed on each side by fluffy drifts of sparkling snow. Remarkably, the glittering, art deco globe hung directly above the conductor's podium with tinsel and frocking was not overdone, but made a savvy, angular accent high above this pretty scene.

Even in Mr. Millson's bleak music department, beauty and creativity was alive and well.

I'd made up my mind, finally, this would be my last concert with the Hillcreek Valley Wind Ensemble, or any of our bands for that matter, and it pained me to see what I was leaving behind was not a complete wasteland.

I watched all these decorations come together from the very

back of the theater. I pondered my exit from the band, and the implied victory it would deliver Mr. Millson, when I realized I hadn't even bothered to assemble my outfit.

Participation in the Winter Formal Concert required a strict, somber uniform. Formal, but not gaudy or distracting. The girls were to wear a black dress with black stockings and black shoes. The boys would wear a black suit, white shirt and tie, and black shoes. The dress code had been explained months ago, in a highly detailed flier posted to the bulletin board, taped to the band room door and pinned throughout the music department hallway.

So it was, the night before the concert, I was calling Mr. Formal to price a dressy pair of size tens.

"Just the shoes?" said the clerk.

"Maybe a pair of pants as well."

"It'll be cheaper if you rent the whole tux."

"I only need the shoes."

"The shoes will run you forty dollars. If you rent the whole tux, it'll only cost seventy more dollars."

"One-hundred and ten dollars?"

"It's a deal!"

"That is not cheaper."

"It is cheaper, on the whole," he urged. "Why spend forty dollars on a pair of shoes, when you can, for just a little more, rent the whole piece?"

My search brought me to the men's department of Value Village. The collection of black dress shoes was not promising.

I was kneeling down, pawing through a rank pile of crusty tennies and boots that promised little more than a scorching case of jungle-rot when I felt someone standing close to me. He was just standing there, smiling down at me, three London Fogs draped over his arm. It was Mr. Millson.

"A raging psychopath?" he asked.

"I'm sorry?" I said, looking up.

"Well," he said. "I guess it's as good a time as any to find yourself a nice pair of black dress shoes. No?"

"Yes!" I said, searching. "Shoes. For the Winter Formal—"

"You know, Barber," he said, with his head cocked to the side. "You're a really talented kid. You've got a head on your shoulders, and if you wanted, you could really be something."

He was circling the drain toward the "but."

"But," he said. "You're a sarcastic punk. A wiseass who never takes anything serious. I see a lot of kids like you and you know what I think?"

I didn't ask—he seemed on the cusp of something memorable, to really let me have it, there in the men's department of the Lynnwood Value Village. I didn't want to spoil his moment.

"I think," he took a small step back and held out his hand, indicating my shoes, pants, shirt then my face. He clapped his hands together like crumpling a piece of trash and tossed it over his shoulder. "A total waste."

"That's fair," I said. "See you tonight!"

We took the stage behind the thick hush of velvet curtains. Each of us tiptoed to our chairs in the dim backlight of the stage, careful not to bang our instrument or music stands. The flutists arranged their dresses over their clasped knees. The brass, all of them, nervously emptied and emptied their instruments with quiet puffs from the spit valves. They ran through a couple last warm-ups, pok-pocking the keys though empty scales and fifths.

Mr. Millson appeared with his great folder, spruced up in a Value Village tux and maybe a couple shots of liquor. His cantaloupe gut poked out from his unbuttoned lapels. He took the conductor's podium, arranged the pile of sheet music and pinched his baton, hiding it behind his back as if accidentally revealing it to the band would inspire an involuntary false start.

He locked in on my black canvas sneakers.

"Barber," he pointed. "Where are your dress shoes?"

There was activity on the other side of those heavy curtains. The theater lights were dimmed and then turned back on: first warning. The audience began their solemn plod from aisles, between rows, to their seats.

"Your shoes!" he hissed. "Where are they?"

"I couldn't find—"

"You had *three months* to find shoes," said someone from the brass section.

One of the stagehands offered a curt "Shh!"

The curtains opened.

Mr. Millson changed his face and turned to the crowd, his hands up to ease the roar of applause. He stepped down from his podium with that signature bobble-head, limp-wristed, jazzy stride and came right up to the edge of the stage to address the crowd. He introduced himself, the band and the pieces for tonight's performance, his toes teetering at the edge of the stage.

His hands flopped around like dangling cold cuts from his sleeves.

He told a couple jokes that were supposed to be funny.

He touched on a serious note, describing a list of the seniors he had the pleasure to work with for four *amazing* years, who wouldn't be joining him next year. I was not on that list.

He finally concluded, looking down to his feet, holding back fake tears (all part of the show) as he turned, and slowly resumed his place at the podium. He opened his great folder, arranged the music again and rapped the baton on his stand. He held the tiny wand, electrifying the air, poised before the flick.

The first strains laid a soft, eerie chill.

The notes were played to near perfection, but without the mechanical passivity of a straight interpretation. There was a cautious, simple vulnerability in the pianissimo, alternately shocked by waves of brass and timpani, pounding time with bulged, weighty crescendos. Their explosive accents laid a solid foundation beneath a polish of chord.

Maybe it was the stage, wound tight with nerves. Maybe it was just Brahms. But for a full three seconds, we were beautiful.

Whatever it was, Mr. Millson cut the trance with a sharp hammering, clacking the baton on his stand. Unsure, the band played on, though crippled. Mr. Millson almost broke this baton as well, until finally the music came to a still.

A murmur spread through the audience. Was this also part of the show?

Mr. Millson apologized to the band. He turned and apologized to the audience, which consisted exclusively of parents and relatives, friends and teachers of everyone on stage.

He apologized again, to the band, for the disruption caused by an obnoxious soloist.

We looked at each other. A soloist?

"Would you like to meet him?" he asked.

He was quiet so the audience couldn't hear. There was a cough, somewhere from the back row.

"Apparently," he continued. "We've been graced by the presence of a soloist."

He clasped his baton behind his back, rocked heel to toe.

"*I said*," he said, "Would you like to meet him?"

He was facing me. Looking down at me.

"Perhaps Nate wouldn't mind standing for the rest of the band?"

Of course, I did not stand. I looked to the only other contrabass clarinetist sitting next to me, Theresa Aylee. Her eyes were bulging, mouth agape. She looked horrified.

"Maybe," he continued. "You might stand and play just your part, as you are so intent on doing anyway? For all of us."

The pause he allowed lasted years. Was I actually playing my part wrong? If anything, I was focused on keeping as quiet as possible. After all, the contrabass clarinet is a real honker. Was it the shoes? Or the vanilla ice cream cone?

Finally, Mr. Millson said, "No? Maybe then you can leave us?"

I said, "I don't want to."

"Take your music, your clarinet and leave the stage."

"No, thank you," I said. "I will stay."

"Would somebody, please, take his clarinet?"

Nobody did. Instead, we waited as if we had all the time in the world.

"Either you can leave the stage," he offered. "Or you can sit there and not play your instrument. It's your choice."

"I will stay."

Mr. Millson tapped his stand again. He would resume the Winter Formal Concert from the top of the piece and, for the first time in four years, he would get to conduct his wind ensemble without me.

"From the top," he said, raising his baton. "Again."

Talent Show

After the Winter Formal Concert, I'd given up exacting my revenge against Mr. Millson. In fact I'm certain, when I finally quit his bands, it was like giving him the best present ever: sweet victory. No matter. The incredible relief, to be rid of it all, was worth it. Maybe all those music dropouts who "couldn't take it" or were "weaklings" were actually far smarter than any of us.

How had I'd been able to stand it? For so long?

It was a mystery.

No matter. My quiet departure from the music department wasn't a moment premature. Even with almost half a school day suddenly freed up, the prospect of completing my remaining credits on time, before summer, was still very uncertain.

So it was, by the middle of my senior year, I was perfectly

absent from the student body. I rarely left the CLIP room. The schedule of bells no longer applied, other than to keep track of the hour. Sometimes I only left for fresh air and a cigarette, or food from the cafeteria, but quickly returned to my packets. I saw nobody, and nobody saw me.

That all changed for Spirit Week, of course.

Not even the janitors were safe from Spirit Week.

Spirit Week was a mix of raucous assemblies, lunch-hour skits from the cheer and flag teams and explosive, impromptu performances by Millson and his marching band. Spirit Week was supposed to get us pumped about our school. Students painted their faces with school colors and dressed themselves in "wacky" outfits. The festivities usually culminated with our football team's trouncing loss in some important game.

Every year, Mr. Millson seized on the frenzied atmosphere of Spirit Week as an implicit invitation to invade various class-rooms with his entire marching band. This was something I'd taken part in numerous times. I used to like it too.

I used to relish the pinned-down panic caused by the sudden introduction of a full marching band to say, French 101 or Second Algebra. One moment, the students were pencil-ing in answers for a multiple choice exam when the doors flew open and in poured thirty-eight kids. All in their flamboyant regalia, armed with sousaphones, trombones, bass drums and crash cymbals.

Before anyone could protest, Mr. Millson would snap off "Ah-one! Ah-two! Ah-one! Two! Three! Four!" and the band unleashed a concussive wall of sound which, in close quarters such as a classroom, could dislodge fillings and pulverize chalk.

We played "Born to be Wild" or "Jungle Fever" or "Barbara Ann," then, as quickly as we'd come, emptied the classroom, ears ringing, lesson plans derailed and trailing a list of complaints that never went further than the vice-principal's desk.

Now it was my turn.

I was hunched over my pile of packet work when the CLIP room doors flew open. In rushed my old marching band. I hadn't seen anyone since the Winter Formal Concert. Then came Mr. Millson, with his trumpet and that ding-dong swagger.

He snapped, "Ah-one, Ah, two! Ah-one, two, three—"

Bethany—God bless her—yelled, "Stop! Stop! Stop!" waving her hands like a heavy seagull. There were stutter-stopping pops and farts from a trombone or saxophone.

She yelled, "What in the good hell...do you think you are doing!?"

It was a rare moment: such a plain, sensible question would have a devastating impact on Mr. Millson and his horrible little universe.

Fizzled in his tracks, Millson offered a feeble, "It's, Spirit Week..."

Normally, provoking the specter of "Spirit Week" was a war cry. A simple excuse for hollering rowdies to go bonkers. Not this time.

Sure, there were some, Theresa Aylee and Sam Kinney, who took the bait and said, "Eep!" with a tiny fist in the air. Everyone else was quiet and still. It is quite a thing, to be surrounded by an unmoving, dead silent marching band.

Mr. Millson simply withered, there's no other way to put it. He withered like fish skin against Bethany, who stood, fists punched into her hips, feet wide. She could have stopped a loco-motive. I followed her example.

This was *our* classroom.

Mr. Millson conspicuously refused to look at me. He eased an off-balance step toward the door, but stopped, guessing he could still slip in at least one, blasting number.

He raised his sad baton. Reflexively, the instruments came up—

"Out!" yelled Bethany. She made a menacing drum major. At once, she took control of Millson's band and marched it in reverse. She called, "Out! Out. Out. Out. Out. Out! Get out! Get out of here!"

The band disarmed, knotted in their ungainly instruments and plugged the doorway. There was an awful clanking and clatter as sousaphones and bass drums jostled for a way, one by one, out the door.

After the long, dreary procession, the door finally closed. Shutting the deflated assembly in the hallway to regroup and lead on, though fatally crippled, to the next unsuspecting classroom.

Bethany brushed off her hands and thumbed over her shoulder at the door, "If that bouffant jackass comes in here again, I'm going to kick his drunk ass."

The marching band departed, minus a snare drummer and cymbalist, my friends Skeeter and Kevin. They stayed behind to catch up. They wanted to know how "special education" was going.

"Great!" I said. "I just finished two years' worth of

requirements! I might even graduate."

"This is your only classroom?"

"Until summer."

"So you didn't notice the talent show is coming up?"

"No."

"We're doing an act," said Kevin.

"It's going to be rad," said Skeeter.

"Millson's going to freak out. He might stop the whole thing and tell us to get off the stage—"

Kevin stopped, remembering the Winter Formal Concert, backtracking, "Aw, man. I'm sorry."

"Yeah," said Skeeter. "You really shit the bed. Is that why you quit—" He snapped, "Wait! I've got it. You should sign up for the talent show!"

I was skeptical. "Don't you have to have talent?"

"Are you kidding?"

They had a point. Every year Mr. Millson lived for that talent show. It was his baby. His chance to showcase all his dearest proteges with him as the spotlit emcee. It was a responsibility he relished as he was free to offer rambling, contemplative half jokes and shaggy-dog witticisms to the high theater lights. He'd go on and on about himself, about his career in jazz and about his legacy as head of Hillcreek Valley High School Music Department.

"It would kill him if you signed up."

I snuck into the band hall during lunch hour, when I thought nobody would be around. It was my first time in the music department since the Winter Formal Concert. I didn't use my name. Instead I signed up as a band, The Nuclear Explosions.

Of course, Mr. Millson was standing right behind me.

"So," he said, swirling his mug. "I see you're signing up for the talent show?"

"Isn't it exciting?" I said. "A little song and dance number. Nothing fancy, just hot jazz. You should like it."

He didn't say anything. He looked into his swirling mug.

Finally, "You know, Barber, a lot of people actually take the talent show seriously."

"I hope so!"

"It's their opportunity to shine. It's their chance to show off their hard work and, of course, their talent."

"Is that why it's called a talent show?"

"It is not, a joke. Or anything to laugh at."

"I hope not!"

He waited.

"So then, you're still signing up?"

"Oh, you betcha!"

"What will you play?"

"I have no idea."

What became of the glut of time recently freed from quitting my music courses?

All it took was the hinting flavor of revenge to suck me right back in. This time, locked up in one of the practice rooms with a collection of instruments pilfered from the music department's generous odds and ends closet.

A lot of people stopped by to look in the window of the small room, curious to see what all the racket was about. When they saw who was in there, they gave a little confirming nod. Eventually I just turned my back on the window and went right on playing, extra loud.

Then there was a knock on the door, which I ignored, until the knocking became pounding. Looking in was Randy Nguyen and two of his teammates from the Eagles' defensive line. All three had helped to make our football team's last two seasons a perfect procession of humiliating losses.

In spite of regularly having their asses handed to them on the field, they still walked the halls of our school with letterman impunity. Their rein of terror was an indiscriminate plow of facepalms, shoulder checks and twisted arms. But it was their suspiciously singular obsession with anyone suspected of homosexuality, their gay fixation, which earned their sad little gang the nickname "Menage au Trois."

They were notorious assholes.

I shrugged and went back to playing the guitar.

The heavy pounding resumed, constant.

"What?!" I yelled, setting down a didgeridoo.

"Come outside for a second," said Randy.

"Why?"

Randy seemed stumped. It was a good question.

The Menage au Trois left the window to have a little huddle.

Randy returned to the window, "We want to ask you a question."

"No thanks," I said, turning back to play the recorder and hammer away on a kick drum. They started pounding and punching the solid door.

"You heard me, faggot," said Randy. "Come on out."

"I'm busy," I said. "Go away."

He put his index finger up, scratching at the air. "Aw, c'mon, buddy. Come outside."

I stepped up to the window, Randy and I were almost nose to nose, aside from the small pane of safety glass.

"I don't wanna."

"That's cool," said Randy. "We'll wait."

I could wait as well. I had all day. I had no classes to attend and a collection of cast-off, broken instruments to learn. As luck would have it, I had a banana and a couple course packets I could work on to pass the time.

One period passed. Two periods. Three.

Normally, the between periods in the music department was a din of rowdiness. Students joked and jostled each other. But the surprise presence of the menacing Menage au Trois shut everyone right up. Everyone hurried past, clutching their sheet music and instruments. No talking. No eye contact. Just flinching dramatically as the occasional punch was pulled.

Another period passed.

The packets turned out to be useless. American History 1945–1960. I'd been reading and rereading the same sentence. Any concentration I could muster went right out that practice room door to the Menage au Trois, hunkered down, waiting for me. I had no appetite for the banana and I'd all but given up trying to tune this stupid zither.

Finally I opened the door.

"At last," said Randy, the Menage au Trois kicking off the wall.

I stepped out to the hallway.

"You're one of those marching band motherfuckers came

into my geometry class to play 'Born to be Wild?'"

"No," I said. "I quit—"

"Fuck you, band geek! I see you at all of our games."

"You like to watch us play football? Queer?"

"You and all the other faggot band geeks."

I didn't argue. What's the use? I waited, as they accused me of this or that until, finally, Randy punched me in the face. He might have broken my nose. Anyway, it hurt enough to drop me to the ground like a sack of meat. The Menage au Trois stood over me, threatening with more if I got up. So I didn't get up.

Eventually they left me alone.

I gathered my books, threw away the smashed banana. My scattered packets would take some rearranging. The two sets of doors, one for the choir room, the other for the band, were each crowded in with three or four faces, some of my former bandmates, all scrambling over each other to catch a peek at the action.

"What happened to your face?!" said my mom. She held my freshly punched face to the light.

"I got hit playing basketball."

My brother craned in to get a good look as well. Of course he'd heard the real story behind my red nose and fat, busted lip. The news had managed to reach him, even though we attended separate schools.

My mom was suspicious.

"I don't think you play basketball," she said. "Do you?"

"Sure I do."

"With who?"

"With...the guys."

"The guys? Who are the guys?"

"Oh," I said. "Skeeter and Kevin."

"Skeeter and Kevin play basketball?"

"No," I said. "They don't."

My brother was enjoying this conversation. He added, "Do you have to get punched in the face before you can play basketball?"

The night of the talent show, just before the curtain went up on the first act, Mr. Millson sidled over to where I was plucking away on a three-string ukulele.

"I'm afraid," he said. "I've some bad news."

"Oh?"

"You signed up as a band?"

"Yes, The Nuclear Explosions."

"Cute. That's just the thing, see. If it's just you, it's a solo act. A solo act can't participate in the band category."

"Why not?"

He crossed his arms, "It's not fair. Everyone else put in the effort to coordinate a group."

"Isn't it?" I said. "Fair?"

"No, it gives you the advantage."

"How so?"

"It just does!" he said.

"Okay, then. I'm a solo act."

"That too," he clucked. "Solo acts are full up. No more allowed."

"Okay, then," I continued. "We're a band. We're The Nuclear Explosions."

"Whatever," he said, finally exhausted. "Your 'band' goes on last."

Mr. Millson took the stage, all smiles, to say how proud he was to introduce the third act, a trio of flautists.

I hurried to go scare up a band and found Skeeter and Kevin in the choir room practicing their kazoos.

"I need a drummer."

They looked at each other, not sure what to do with this news.

"Mr. Millson won't let me go on if The Nuclear Explosions is just me."

"That sucks," said Skeeter. "What are you going to do?"

"Convince one of you guys to join The Nuclear Explosions."

They both cocked a head, like curious collies.

"Whaddya say?"

"No," said Skeeter.

Who could blame him?

Kevin said, "Sure! I'll do it."

"I have to warn you."

"Yes?"

"This is going to be bad."

"Right."

"Like, awful."

"Okay."

"Like terrible, bad. And it will go on and on and on—"

"Okay, okay. How long?"

"I suppose, until Millson kicks us off the stage."

The act Mr. Millson introduced as "The Highwayman" walked to the microphone stand at the center of the stage. He wore squeaky black cowboy boots, solid black jeans and a starched dark purple shirt with a black bolo tie. He wore a cowboy hat with a brim so wide the stage lights cast his whole face and broad shoulders in shadow.

Football rowdies yelled from their clutch in the audience, "FAAAAG!"

He nodded his big hat to the sound booth. The music began, soft piano, the opening strains of "Desperado."

The Highwayman sang the first note, and when his voice came, everyone just stopped. He didn't move at all, just stood there with a dumb thumb hung in a belt loop, the other hand gripping the microphone somewhere under that giant hat. He dipped the hat to pause, then wrung another lush, honeyed verse.

As the song faded to close, the house came down around him. Everyone was on their feet, screaming. Even I was standing and clapping wildly.

He removed his hat, the big reveal: underneath that wide brim was Randy Nguyen, pouring sweat. He stepped back and took a gracious bow and slipped under the hat again. Even after he stepped off stage, the crowd was still standing, shouting for an encore. Even his teammates.

Mr. Millson took the microphone with his notecards, his hands up against the violent applause.

"Thank you, thank you—" he said. "Thank you!"

The crowd finally settled, took their seats.

He peered at his notes, "There's a promising career in karaoke for that one there. The Highwayman—Mr. Randy Nuh-Goy-en, everyone. Randy Nuh-Guy-Something-Or-Other."

Crickets.

Mr. Millson spent maybe five whole minutes fawning over the next act, another gaggle of flautists.

"I want you all to know," he continued, choking back tears. "How much of a pleasure—" *choke* "a true privilege it has been to instruct these fine girls. Let's give them a good standing ovation, okay? Everyone?"

Scattered applause. Nobody stood.

The girls took the stage like a litter of kittens in a strange new environment. Mr. Millson said something to them, urgent and off-mic, herding them clumsily to the front of the stage, for a halting, uncertain bow.

He said, "Take it away, kids!"

When it came to the last act, The Nuclear Explosions, Mr. Millson introduced us as the "Unclear Explosive."

I took the stage with my instruments: a twenty-foot length of pipe and rattling, dusty old guitar, which, since the last time I'd seen it leaning against the wall backstage, had mysteriously lost its low E string. The string was not broken, but had been clipped clean off.

Maybe someone was trying to screw things up for The Nuclear Explosions?

Little did they know!

Kevin threw at the drums, working them into an instant lather. The tempo was a little too fast, but I couldn't complain. This was, after all, the first we'd ever played together. I'm just glad he happened to choose the right time signature. I was lucky, he was such a sport.

With the drums in a crashing, rolling boil, I tucked into the chords that may or may not have been the correct chords to the Everly Brothers, "Let It Be Me." No matter, the sheer volume was impressive enough.

The solo took a bit of doing. The microphone had to be placed, just so, at the end of the twenty-foot pipe, which I accidentally kicked and sent rolling toward the audience. I played it out, like this was all part of the act.

Once I'd made the journey back to the other end of the pipe and rolled it back to the microphone on the floor, half the audience had walked out, which was unfortunate because the one glorious honk that honked from the other end of that pipe was the kiss of death for the whole theater's sound system. That was the solo.

Speakers buzzing and cutting out, we finished the set with an indulgent freakout, brought home by the sizeable cut on my lip from the sharp edge of pipe. I was bleeding freely.

It was all part of the act.

The end of the school year, I turned in my last three packets with a warning.

"American History," I told Bethany. "1945–1960. It has blood on it."

She took the packets.

"That's odd," she said. "Most people are quite romantic about America's postwar years."

"And some banana," I said.

I waited as she and Laura checked through the packets. Two came in at a B-plus, and one was an A-minus. All three were "fails" since I'd pre-selected their grades to be an A.

"I can correct the mistakes!" I begged. "I still have time."

"No," said Bethany. "You have everything *except* for time."

"On the other hand," said Laura. "Whatever that was at the talent show? I can assure you, nobody's holding their breath for next year's encore."

She handed me the packets.

"I'm sorry."

And that was that.

I took the bloodied, crumpled packets across the school to my counselor, Maurine Clark. I'd already ordered and paid for my commencement gown and cap and was thinking of how expensive that was when Maurine, on the phone, motioned for me to take the seat in front of her desk.

"No, he's here now," she said to the phone. "Three? Dang, that's close. What were the grades?"

Maurine waited, listening.

"But he chose A's?"

She put her palm against the receiver and mouthed, "It'll be just a second."

Just a second.

Everybody's got plenty of time. Everyone except for me. I would be coming back for a fifth year of high school. I melted into my seat at the very thought of it. I was on the verge of fainting to this half of their conversation—Maurine and Bethany casually discussing my future.

Maurine set the phone in its cradle and laced her fingers. She leaned in and said, "Well!"

The first day of school I stalked around the music department with my corrected packets. I was caked in dirt and sunburnt, on lunch break from my construction job.

I peeked into the band room door.

There were a couple students milling about, old friends catching up after an eventful summer.

The head of the music department, Mr. Millson, was in his office in a reclining high-back chair. He cradled his mug on the tummy shaped like a perfect cantaloupe. Some kids said "excuse me" as they slipped past me for their first day of band. They must've been freshman. I didn't know anybody there, and nobody knew me.

Mr. Millson took a wincing pull from his mug and returned the beverage to its paunchy cradle. He leaned back in his chair to admire the view out his window.

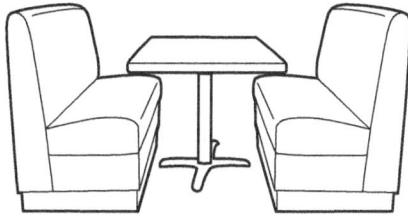

Morbid Curiosity

Shepherd, show me how to go
O'er the hillside steep,
How to gather, how to sow,
How to feed Thy sheep.
I will listen for Thy voice,
Lest my footsteps stray;
I will follow and rejoice
All the rugged way.
　　　　　—Mary Baker Eddy

Against the advice of my lawyer and stern warnings from my therapist, I accepted Elsbeth's invitation to lunch. Even though I knew what she was going to say: the unsayable. I wanted to hear her say it, to look her in the eyes and watch her say it.

I, on the other hand, had nothing to say. What else was

there to say, this late in the case?

This was toward the end of my lawsuit against Howard, after everyone had been deposed. When everything had been said and repeated until even the most fantastical, unbelievable turns in the four years I worked for Howard became a droll recitation of cold dates and names. We'd entered a lull in these last few months. With the date for the hearing still two months out, both our lawyers took to their offices, preparing to either settle out of court or for the much-dreaded alternative of going to trial. For everyone else, there was an eerie, waiting calm.

This was a notorious quiet stage for these types of cases. The waiting lends, naturally, to a simmering panic. Both sides get restless and usually do something stupid. This is how so many perfectly sound civil cases go belly-up.

In this restlessness, her invitation arrived: a sad, thinly veiled Hail Mary, cooked up likely without the consent of Howard's lawyer. It said she wanted to enjoy a lunch. To offer counsel as a friend. Two things we'd never shared before the trial, which now conspicuously betrayed her true intentions— to convince me to drop the case.

Elsbeth's role in our case was nothing new. It is not uncommon that someone trusted, a parent even, would side with the accused, in spite of the monstrous things they'd done. This for a number of reasons. A desperate mind is an acrobat at rationalization. Most commonly a man in Howard's position would have flatly denied every accusation I'd leveled against him and that would be all she needed to believe none of this ever happened, enough to conclude I'd lost my mind or was just after his money. Or, in cases where the evidence was overwhelming, I'd be just another spurned fag out for love-sick revenge. The peculiar twist to our case, which ceaselessly frustrated Howard's lawyer and surprised everyone including myself, was that Howard, her long-time friend and business partner, cinched this common loophole by uniformly agreeing with every accusation I'd leveled against him.

This put Elsbeth, and that acrobat brain of hers, in a real tight spot.

In spite of my better judgement, I was compelled still, led by an awful curiosity to hear her say it, to look her in the eyes and watch her say it.

I arrived early at Jimbo's Family Restaurant—a campy, neon monument to greasy diners on the corner of 196th and Highway 99 which, as the true heart of Lynnwood, was appropriately clogged with traffic. I spent the extra time watching the Jimbo's sign.

While I lived here my whole life and passed this corner countless times, this was my first good look at the sign.

"Jimbo's Family Restaurant: *Our food is cooked, just for you.*" As far as appetizing slogans, this was right in line with the tire emporiums, the grease monkeys and junkyards that littered the crusty shoulders of Highway 99. A motto was supposed to whet the appetite. Jimbo's offered little more than to clarify their food's temperature, it's destination.

Nike: The shoes go on your feet.

Apple: For computing.

Ford: It's transportation.

Then again, this was Lynnwood: a gamey suburb north of

Seattle whose people would instinctively whiff condescension in anything fancier than *"Our food is cooked, just for you."*

Lynnwood: suburbs with people.

Elsbeth's small blue Chrysler pulled off the highway and parked next to my car. I often wondered how this very moment would unfold, after—everything. So it was a surprise when she opened her arms for a big hug. I met her with a step back, a dry handshake.

We shook hands.

It was chilly out, and Elsbeth clutched her mauve vinyl purse to her chest with her bony, arthritic fingers. Her eyelids never really opened when she was speaking to you.

"Thank you for meeting me," she said, fluttering her eyes. "It has been too long. I hope you're doing well?"

"Oh yeah," I said. "Super duper."

Elsbeth looked down Highway 99. Maybe clocking an escape route.

"Shall we lunch?" I asked, leading the way to the door.

"That would be fine," she said, eyes closed. "Yes."

I might've been the only one in my family who thought it was inappropriate Elsbeth would open our front door without knocking.

At first, she was just the nosey busybody who lived across the street. Her first impositions were only here and there, to vacuum the living room, or wash the dishes as a favor to my mother. She said Mom needed all the help in the world because Dad was gone so often. Soon she was freely scolding my sisters and my brother and me for not helping out as much as we should. There was a household to run, after all. Our house wasn't going to clean itself.

Her own house was, of course, spotless.

Dust-free wall sculptures. Marbled, ice-blue carpet, vacuumed daily, filled the living room and rippled down the long hall of the rambler to each of her daughters' immaculately vacant rooms. Her husband, Hal never moved from his La-Z-Boy, parked in front of the television smoking cigarette after cigarette. When lunch or dinner rolled around, Elsbeth would shuffle out with a TV tray full of hot food, and make sure Hal had his napkin and salt and pepper.

Sometimes, I would see them, through their wide picture window, eating together. Elsbeth nudged close to the La-Z-Boy with a TV tray of her own, chewing in unison with Hal.

Eventually, she convinced Mom we should be attending church, and she was just the one to take us. Additionally, this would give Mom Sunday mornings to herself.

It took ages to get us four, wiry kids dressed and out the door. Elsbeth, not being one to wait for children to organize themselves, simply barged in the house and shooed after us this way or that until we were dressed and out the door.

Routines like this let way to further impositions. Once I walked past our bathroom and almost jumped right out of my skin to see Elsbeth out of the corner of my eye. She was kneeling in front of our toilet wearing yellow gloves, scouring the porcelain bowl like crazy. I thought I was the only one at home. Everyone else was down at the park.

"And where are you headed?" she wanted to know.

I told her I was looking for something, a toy my brother

had misplaced, or hid on purpose. Anyway, it was lost and I was going nuts looking for it.

"Well," she said, smacking the scrub brush on the edge of the toilet, flushing. "Stop your dawdling, and say, 'Shepherd.' If it's here, we'll find it. We'll say 'Shepherd,' together."

She peeled off the yellow gloves, turned them right side out and placed them under the bathroom sink, herding me into my room.

"Now, what does this—toy, look like?"

"It's a car," I said. "Small, red."

"Where did you see it last?"

"I can't remember—"

"You *do* remember. Now think, if this is such an important toy, where was it last seen?"

I pointed to my bedside shelf, "Here?"

"Fine," she said. "Now, say 'Shepherd' with me—"

Reciting the poem made me cringe, but I said it anyway, repeating the words over and over as I looked through the drawers of my beside table, to the dresser, through the dresser drawers, the closet. Elsbeth went through my brother's side of the room, his drawers, his shelves of books and toys after the elusive red car.

She checked the time. She wore her small watch backwards, so the face nestled the inside of her wrist. She clucked at the dial, upset we'd already spent this much time looking for a toy. Here she was, hijacking what had been a lazy summer day and a couple moments to myself and *she* was the one getting angry. Her mounting frustration was making her frantic as she wailed about the loss of otherwise productive time, marveling out loud about children and their toys, the wastefulness of it all.

"Mark my words," she said from under my brother's bed. "One day you will work for a living of your own and you will rue the time you've wasted on toys."

I shouted at her, "Why are you even in our house!"

Her rump stopped shuffling around. She hurried to extricate herself from under the bed. She came at me but stopped, her sweater billowing with dust bunnies. She was horrified, shocked speechless and would have hit me if she weren't already on the verge of tears.

"*What did you just say?*"

I repeated what I'd said, and so very much more. I called her wicked names and told her to leave me alone and get out of our house. When she did just that, I realized my grave error. Of course, as soon as she saw Mom come home, she called to rat me out. Mom's face drained to the tinny tirade on the other line. She hung up the phone and marched me straight across the street by my neck and stood me in front of Elsbeth to convince her, if I could, to forgive me. Somehow.

Elsbeth, eyebrows raised, eyes closed, shook her head and said, "Well, I never." She'd never heard a child talk like that. To an an elder no less, except the one time when her daughter came home from school and declared she had to "use the can" before dinner. As for forgiveness, it was the Christian thing to do, but she would have to think about it.

Suddenly, the volume on *Wheel of Fortune* came roaring from the TV. Hal, holding the remote and a cigarette, wheezed from the La-Z-Boy, "*Do you mind?*"

Elsbeth and I waited in the restaurant lobby, as the sign requested, to be seated.

We said nothing. We must have looked downright miserable to be there, waiting to be greeted by the hostess, who led us through a maze of people enjoying their meals. Then negotiating the prospect of settling in a seat or booth, thanking the hostess. The whole obnoxious charade only accentuated the agonizing distance between these niceties and the real, awful reason we were there.

We opened our menus, feigning interest in any number of dishes. The menu was decorated with pictures of specialty platters, but they all looked like nauseating slop.

"The Reuben looks good," I lied.

Elsbeth looked up. "The what?"

"The Reuben, though, I don't like rye bread, so maybe they can substitute the rye for sourdough…"

"Or," she said, returning to her menu. "Whole wheat. It's healthier. Better yet, a salad. You're off to college in a week? You'll have to learn how to eat healthier than a Reuben."

I was going to win the lawsuit, there was no question about that. The only question was how badly it would end for Howard.

I thought, starting out, I would get maybe a couple hundred dollars and follow up with a criminal trial to send Howard to jail. Three months into the case, my lawyer finally admitted there would be no criminal trial.

"You can't have both," he said flatly. "The good news is, we're not talking about a couple hundred dollars here." He laughed. "That's for small claims."

He chucked my shoulder, "I don't know if you know this,

Nate, but there's potential you'll make a million dollars here."

"I think," said Elsbeth. "I'll get the house salad. I don't remember everything being so expensive!"

"But," I said. "The house salad is so boring! It's a pile of iceberg lettuce with carrot shreds, crunchy water and dressing."

"On the side," she said, finger up, eyes closed. "They always put too much dressing when it's on the salad."

"That's hardly a lunch."

"And some tea."

Of course, what my lawyer had meant to say, was he would potentially win a third of a million dollars for representing my open-and-close case.

I was still young enough to not yet know my lawyer was just as much a predator as Howard. That chummy shoulder-chuck was just grooming.

Years later, it would turn out, that same lawyer would be disbarred and prosecuted for tampering with evidence in a case strikingly similar to mine. Except, he was representing the guilty party. That case, two years in the making, was thrown out for mistrial and had to be restarted from the ground up.

"I wasn't sure you'd accept my invitation," she said, finally. "I'm glad you did."

"I was hesitant, obviously. But I have nothing to hide."

"Good. We can meet here, without the lawyers. We can cut through all this nonsense and just sit and work this out."

There was quiet. We looked out the window at traffic rushing by on 99.

Elsbeth wondered, "What color do you think the Puget

Sound is today?"

"Elsbeth, I need to tell you—"

"You remember when I drove you home from church? Every Sunday. And when we passed the Edmonds Ferry? Before you could see the Sound, I'd point to the sky and say, 'If the sky is that color, what color do you suppose the Puget Sound would be?'"

"Yes. I remember. It's not a very hard question Elsbeth. The Puget Sound, maybe all bodies of water for that matter, are the same color as the sky. One reflects the other."

"That's true!" blinked Elsbeth, clasping her hands together. She seemed wonderfully satisfied I'd been able to grasp this marvelously simple concept she'd managed to impart. At least one of the many lessons she'd repeated and repeated, for better or worse, stuck.

She was still beaming, out the window, maybe remembering those bucolic Sunday drives with my brother and me, home from church. She was still swept by the memory, the peach-warm glow of an Edmond's sunrise when I told her, "I need you to know, Elsbeth. Out of the gate, here. I will not be dropping the lawsuit."

She deflated from the window. "Then what did you come here for?"

"To be honest?" I said. "Morbid curiosity."

Eyes closed. "Well. I'm just... surprised at you, Nate. That's rather... cruel. Isn't it?"

"Is it?" I asked. "You're familiar with the case. They took your deposition. I read that deposition. Just as you read Howard's deposition. You had it for a week."

"I would not," eyelids fluttering, hands up. "Read anything like...*that*."

"But you're aware of what the case is about—"

She batted at the air. "You don't need to go over it! And for God's sake, not here."

I asked, "Do you know why I suggested we meet here? At Jimbo's?"

Startled, she clutched her hands. "Honestly? No."

I reminded her of the night, long ago, when my mom let my brother and me stay at her house for a sleepover. She brought us to Jimbo's for dinner. It was a positively Norman Rockwellian meal.

"Do you remember what happened that night?"

"No," she said suspicious. Likely it was this case, the grueling depositions, that made her leery of leading questions.

"I found a slice of your daughter's wedding cake, under her bed. It must have been ten years old, or more."

"Oh, yes," she laughed, relieved. "Haha! I remember now, you were screaming? You ate some, yes?"

"I polished off the whole slice, yes."

She laughed hard, into her hands.

"That's why I chose Jimbo's," I said.

She stopped, stung. "I don't follow."

I told her the real reason I came. I told her I'd read and re-read her lengthy deposition. How, in spite of the overall interview, its thoroughness left a nagging disbelief. I told her all of this, to her face. To call her out as the breathtaking contradiction she represented and how it was driving me crazy to just let it go, as my therapist and so many others suggested I do. How, the only way around it was to witness it for myself. Face to face. I pointed out her pitying expression, the cool and steady stir she gave to an already well-stirred cup of tea, and how I'd plainly made a horrible mistake. There was no question, in spite of our long history, whose team she was on.

She continued to stir her tea, back and forth. She used a spoon to cup and cradle the teabag, winding its string around the bag, to squeeze the remaining drip into her mug. She placed the spoon aside and picked up the cup, cradling it to warm her hands.

"I have to say," she finally said. "I am not impressed. Not at all. In fact, I'm disappointed in you. Honestly, I expected more from you. This whole thing is the devil. That's how he works. Remember, 'judge not, lest ye be judged.' And you can believe, Howard will face the Lord. Just as you will. That is one thing that is true."

I realized my mouth was hanging open and shut it.

She went on, "When you put your trust in the Lord—"

"What then," I asked. "About speeding tickets? Shoplifting?"

She brushed it aside, shaking her head.

"And child abuse and fraud? Are we to allow people free reign with the idea that God will dole out their appropriate punishment? What, then, is our entire judicial system for?!"

"What I'm saying is, it's not for you."

"So—even with everything," I continued dumbly. "Our past, and everything you were to our family, a friend and guardian, a trusted role that you failed—"

"Nate," she said. "You told me why you came here, fine.

Now, I'll tell you why I came here. Okay? I came here today because I wanted you to know: *I forgive you.*"

She was blinking furiously now.

"And I do, Nate. I forgive you! For—you know not what you are doing. Which is the devil's work. You're doing it for him! And I hope you see how you have the chance, now. To do the right thing. The Christian thing. Say 'Shepherd,' good and long, and you will come to see the right thing to do is to drop this case—"

Just then, as if by the good grace of God, our food arrived.

The summer between eighth and ninth grade, Elsbeth, always keen to find work for idle hands, suggested I work with her for a weekend. That was the weekend of the Seattle Gift Show. She and Howard ran a booth that required no small amount of work to put together and staff. Especially since the boys they could normally count on refused to participate this year.

The booth was actually Howard's, as was the business. Elsbeth was just his assistant and bookkeeper. Together, they ran a nick-nackery, filling orders and shipments of small ceramic creatures: seals, bears, beavers and dolphins. All this was completed from Howard's run-down house in Northgate.

This was when the internet was still the fledgling World Wide Web, so the gift show was their only opportunity to display all the sets and individual figurines for collectors and owners of beach-town novelty shops and kitschy gift stores.

She wasn't kidding about the work. Each box was precisely packed with the ceramic critters, each wrapped in delicate tissue, then newspaper. They were packed and transported and painstakingly displayed and then babysat for three days by either Elsbeth or Howard or me. It was an incredibly busy affair (I had no idea people were so bonkers for tchotchkes!), we disassembled the booth, returned all the creepy animals into the tissue, then newspaper, then box, then truck and then back to Howard's house.

We were unloading the last of the boxes when Elsbeth approached me with my check. It was late at night.

As their bookkeeper, it was her responsibility to pay me for the fair amount of work I'd completed. She held it back, unsure I should be paid. Of course, she conceded the check, but not without conditions: I had to promise, her and Howard, I would spend their money wisely.

It would turn out, they were so impressed with the work I did that weekend, I was hired. A few days later, Elsbeth appeared in our dining room to give me the good news, though, she admitted, she was not happy about the wage Howard set: five dollars an hour. A dollar more than my trial period that busy weekend. She said Howard liked me a lot, so it was a shameless bribe. She maintained I should have *earned* that raise. Children only throw away the money they don't earn.

She continued, "You can work. You've got the job if you want it. On the condition it's okay with your mother. Of course, I'll be there," Elsbeth said, reassuringly. "To keep an eye on you, if you need anything. Anything at all."

The next part is the part where we're supposed to eat all this food we ordered. Which we tried but two nauseating bites in, I asked the waitress for a to-go box.

Our food was untouched, a prop. Our conversation was over. It was the last we'd ever speak. We sat across the table from each other, waiting for the check, saying nothing. Elsbeth, fingers laced over her purse, watched the traffic stop and go down Highway 99. North, south. Soot gray and threatening to snow.

The Skirt

Crossing your legs, it turns out, is a whole other ball game when you're wearing a skirt. I discovered this bit of trivia in the front office, waiting for the vice-principal to call me in. Dorothy, the head secretary with pursed, disapproving lips was giving me the hard stink eye as I fidgeted with my legs. She wore narrow reading glasses perched at the tip of her nose. A long gold chain draped from its hinges. She cast her obvious looks first over the narrow frames then, tipping her head back, open mouthed, to size me up. Her penciled eyebrows sailed this way and that over a forehead as wide and shiny as a platter of heavily buttered mashed potatoes.

She finished this dramatic scowl with a deep, exaggerated sigh, announcing simply, "Kids."

I shot back, "What?!"

She gave a snooty shoulder tick and a sniff and went back

to shuffling paperwork.

Actually it was my sister's skirt, and not a very feminine skirt at that. It was more like hippy drapes with a tassel and two charms dangling from the elastic waistband. I could have chosen something smaller, a mini skirt even, but I wasn't committed enough to shave my legs. Also, I didn't have the right shoes.

Even if Dorothy had bothered to ask, I doubt the logical reasoning behind this more sensible, floor-length number would have impressed her much. I caught her gassing off another cartoonish sigh, shaking head and her wrinkled bags of jowl.

Recently, a controversial bulletin had been published in our school paper, the *Eagle Eye*. It was written by our vice-principal, Mr. Allen. Mr. Allen's hair was either permed or naturally frizzy. For a white guy it was a robust, not-ironic afro which was punctuated on the crown by a clear, perfectly shaped bald patch. The haircut had earned him the nickname "Donut 'Fro."

"Did you see?" fumed Ian. "What Donut 'Fro posted in the *Eagle Eye*?"

He had a copy and pushed it for me to read.

The bulletin was an update on appropriate dress code for boys and girls. Among the usual requests was an additional challenge: "Boys shall not wear skirts or dresses to school or sanctioned functions."

The modest request did not go unnoticed. After all, we lived in the suburbs where there was a dearth of predators and not a lot of anything else to think about. We were, of course, uniformly outraged. The indignation, at least among my circle of friends, percolated to a hubbub until it became obvious—somebody needed to make a stand.

Perhaps too quickly, I came to the conclusion—that somebody should be me.

I'd decided our staid social norms were ripe for violent upheaval and I would be its provocateur. The first to thumb my nose at timeless faux pas, sedentary normalcy and the nebulous "establishment," and on and on.

During the bus ride to school the next day, I felt like a genuine activist. I could feel everyone looking at me: a boy wearing a skirt! I happily caught their looks and returned them with a hot glare. I wanted them to feel uncomfortable. Those whose attention I was able to snare did certainly worm in their seats.

Or maybe they were just shifty because there was a boy over there, in a skirt, desperately trying to stare them down.

The main entrance to Hillcreek Valley High was a wide set of doors with tinted, almost mirrored glass that offered the student body a good last look before committing to the day. Kids often loitered at these cruel mirrors to either fluff up or recoil at their risky new haircut, or daring, adventurous ensemble. It was here the revolutionary luster of that dowdy skirt seemed suddenly clownish. I longed for the refuge of a familiar pair of jeans like never before.

There was no way around it, I looked ridiculous.

I swallowed back, opened the door and made my way inside.

I casually sidled up to my circle of friends whose reactions, ranging from repellent shock to uncontrollable laughter, were similarly nonreassuring.

"What are you doing?" shot Ian, almost offended. "You're going to get in *trouble!*"

Alicia announced, hands up, "I'm outta here." Even my good friend Stephanie slithered away after her.

Was everyone suddenly overcome with amnesia? Where was their anger? Where was the dress-code outrage that had sent us into throes of activism?

I couldn't even hide my hands since that stupid skirt wasn't equipped with pockets.

I just stood there, with my dumb hands, hemorrhaging friends and wondering about the sadist who'd design a lower garment *without pockets.*

After the humiliating pageant that was lunch hour, I was officially over it. I decided to skip the rest of school, bus straight home and never, ever ever, turn my back on a good pair of pants again. There was an assembly in the theater and I planned to escape after its dismissal in the shuffle of students returning to class.

The assembly was a demonstration by a man who called himself Mr. Science. He'd brought his robot, BOBBI, for a demonstration.

As we entered the theater, the robot was doing a twirl and whistling a little tune, a precursor for the main event. The robot, it turned out, was not autonomous. It wasn't even unplugged. It was more of a remote appendage, tethered to Mr. Science by a thick umbilical of heavy untwistable cables and pneumatic tubing. Mr. Science stayed to the edge of the stage, controlling

BOBBI's jerky movements and making him talk by way of a cumbersome remote panel and headset.

The theater went dark and Mr. Science took center stage, throwing an arm around the robot in the spotlight.

"Greetings, science lovers!" he boomed. "Welcome...to the FUTURE!"

He introduced us to the robot whose name, BOBBI, was an acronym for something that made no sense. We were warned that BOBBI would be our competition in whatever grim, mechanized workforce awaited us after high school. Jobs that, until now, had largely been performed by human people. Manufacturing and assembly, the service industry and even driving our larger cities' taxis. We were implored to imagine a future in which nuclear disasters like Chernobyl, where a blast site was too toxic for people, could be investigated, cleaned and repaired by legions of tiny BOBBIs.

"Imagine!" said the scientist, making his way to the controls again. "A time when bank robberies are a thing of the past."

He picked up a squirt gun and pointed it at BOBBI.

"Stick 'em up! This is a robbery!"

BOBBI shrugged his shoulder sockets and rested its pincers on its waist section.

Then, instead of surrendering the make-believe money, as a human teller would be compelled, the robot stood on its tiptoe-wheels and did a little cheeser and shrug to the audience before launching into a dance routine to 2 Unlimited's "Get Ready for This."

There was even a light show, but the crowd was largely

unimpressed. We only laughed mildly when BOBBI demonstrated his moonwalk, which was just rolling backward to Michael Jackson's "Don't Stop 'till You Get Enough."

Finally, after his cute routine, Mr. Science aimed BOBBI at the crowd and said through the robot, "*Mmmm* can I have a volunteer to the stage *mmmm?*"

Nobody raised their hands.

"*Mmmm* come on. *Mmm* there's got to be one brave soul out there?"

Still, no hands. Then BOBBI said, "*Mmm* where is the boy in the dress?"

The house lights came up.

"*Mmm* I thought I saw a pretty boy in a dress—"

Someone behind me shouted, "Here! He's here!"

BOBBI zeroed in on me, "*Mmm* come on down, kid. *Mmmm* let's see what you're *mmm*ade of."

I hissed at the group of boys egging me on, but dutifully took the aisle to the stage, leading with my chin. Nothing weird here. Nothing to be ashamed of.

At the steps to the stage, I gathered my skirt in a bunch. This was only a practical measure, to avoid stepping on the hem while mounting the stairs. Everyone thought this was just hilarious. BOBBI thought it was hilarious as well. He turned to the crowd and minced back and forth, "*Mmm*—Oooh la-laaah," it droned. Everyone laughed and laughed.

I was already super funny, and we hadn't even begun.

"*Mmm* what's your name?" said BOBBI.

"My name is Nate."

"*Mmm* nice to meet you *Nn*natalie," said BOBBI. He did a

little robo-curtsy, reaching out to kiss my hand.

Laughter, applause.

"*Mmm*," said BOBBI to the audience. "That's a very nice dress."

He shook one of his little pincers and imitated a wolf whistle.

"It's a skirt," I said, sticking out my chin. "Thank you very much."

Light music began to play over the sound system, the opening strains of "The Blue Danube."

"*Mmm* Natalie. Do you like to dance?"

"I do not."

"Would you like to dance with me?"

"No."

"*Mmm* come on," BOBBI said, resting a pincer on the small of my back. "I'll take the lead."

He winked a shutter to the crowd and they went wild.

"No!" I said. "I don't want—" Its claws were already around me, pushing me backwards. We lurched to the side. Oily puffs of air hissed and popped from its hydraulic joints as BOBBI groaned and lunged clumsily to the swirling crescendo. I pushed back against the robot but it was as solid as a Chevrolet.

Again, it pressed forward and I fumbled backward in its poking, mechanical grasp. In the stumble, the hem of my skirt caught between the floor and one of BOBBI's wheels, and the skirt pulled free and clear from my waist to a sad rumple around my feet. I was wearing white briefs, creepy and utilitarian, but far better than if I'd chosen to go commando: a direction I'd momentarily debated before heading out the door that morning.

The crowd erupted in a roar as Johann Strauss's cymbals crashed. I frantically wrestled my skirt from the gear and tracks of BOBBI's wheels when, to my horror, I felt its cold claw on my back, moving downwards.

"*MmmMm*," whistled robo-pervert. "That was delightful—"

Everyone, even the teachers, were in an uproar.

Finally, I yanked the skirt loose and I slapped BOBBI on what would have been its cheek.

"Get your fucking meathooks off of me!" I shouted. "You fucking faggot!"

Everyone, mid-clap, was suddenly silent. Everyone except for Johann Strauss and his grotesquely florid waltz, sauntering forward, despite the ugly turn our performance had taken. I gathered the skirt around my waist and ran for the door, where my drama teacher, a former drill instructor for the Marines, was stationed like a brick wall.

"No way, Barber," he said solidly. "To the office."

Of course everyone heard this, in spite of "The Blue Danube," and the chorus of laughter returned. I was funny again.

"Mr. Allen will see you now," said Dorothy, ominously extending her flappy arm to his door, the hand limp.

Donut 'Fro was standing at his window, hands clasped, back to the doorway. His weird bald patch gleamed from its bushy nest. He rocked from heel to toe, saying nothing as I took a seat. I fumbled to cross my legs until I just gave up and waited.

Without turning away from the window he said, "I heard about what happened."

People even called him "Donut 'Fro" directly, as he was increasingly good humored, funny even, as he approached the end of the year, his last before retirement.

As the door closed, his jocular impersonation crisped with gravity.

"Let's begin," he sighed, stopping, finally turning from the window. He eased into his chair like it was a hot tub, "Let's begin with the skirt."

"What about it?" I charged.

"I assume this is in retaliation to our updated dress code?"

"I don't know what you're talking about," I said.

"Whatever," said Mr. Allen.

He thought better of the chair, standing up again. He returned to the window, which looked over the large track and football field. It was certainly a delightful view. If it were my view, I might've spent a good amount of time admiring it as well. Especially when a conversation such as ours was the alternative.

Our campus was only three years old then. It had been an impressive remodel with many featured extravagances. From the gigantic theater, a yawning cafeteria and event hall to spacious, waxed hallways lined with stoic, block lockers. Its design and construction cost a tidy sum, which leveled a hefty bond measure on the community and a hard fight to clear with the district board.

Mr. Allen seemed to be mulling all this over, as well as his fast approaching retirement. He maneuvered to his point.

"As you know, boys aren't allowed to wear skirts or dresses here, or at sanctioned functions."

"What about high heels?"

"What about them?" he shrugged.

"Can boys wear high heels?"

"It's your funeral."

"So what's the difference?"

"High heels and skirts, you will notice, are not the same item—"

"What about kilts?!"

"Ah yes," he said tiredly, as if he'd predicted this part of the conversation. "The old kilts-are-skirts argument." He stopped. "Listen, we asked you politely. A simple, modest request which you directly, and tastelessly I might add, disobeyed."

"But this dress code," I insisted. "Only reinforces gender stereotypes! It only breeds homophobia—"

"Ah, yes," he held one finger in the air. "I'm glad you mentioned that, since this unfortunate event at the robotics demonstration..."

"That—" I said, "that wasn't my fault."

"No? You didn't call BOBBI a..." he picked up a piece of paper from his desk and tilted back to read it, mouth open. "An 'effing faggot?'"

"Yes, I said that, but-—"

"BOBBI is," he looked from the paper to me, still through the glasses. "A *robot*. No?"

"He was pushing me and touching me!"

I lit into my side of the story: the unsolicited advances, the wolf-whistling. I told him about the waltz and how my skirt just disappeared and my briefs—

"One could argue," he said, taking off his glasses to massage the bridge of his nose, "you're unfamiliar with waltzing in floor-length skirts?"

"So is robot-waltzing part of our core curriculum now?!" I beamed. I was really on a roll.

Mr. Allen finished massaging his face. It left him ruddy and puffy-eyed, and he seemed on the verge of sliding into a narcotic nod. He looked, suddenly, so old.

I wondered about a younger Mr. Allen, as he was just beginning his career in education with a full, healthy afro. Certainly he heard plenty of horror stories from his friends and relatives about the challenges he would face in education. Until now, he appeared to have taken it all in stride. Until now, when he seemed so instantly ancient, and tired and even betrayed that I'd managed to slip in this stupid conversation so late in his career, just as he was certain he had it all figured out.

The Pants

The pants had become an obsession.

I found them while shopping for hair bleach and dye. I was moping between racks of clothing and shoes, half admiring everything I couldn't afford. Suddenly I was confronted by two mannequins, posing as if on a street corner, wearing identical pairs of red Scottish plaid pants.

The pants were crisscrossed with buckles and rows of zippers—strictly for show because the buckles could not be undone and the zippers only unzipped to reveal the absence of pockets. The pants even came with a pair of sewn-in suspenders, also just for show. The grumpy mannequins, complete with mohawks and menacing expressions, frozen in defiant snarls, demonstrated how the suspenders were meant to dangle like drapery about the thighs.

One of the mannequins, the one squatting and ready to

pounce, betrayed a poor design in these purely decorative suspenders. As he was crouching, both straps dangled below the heel of his boots, mopping to the ground. Extricating himself from this position, to stand, say, would require gathering his danglings clear of the boots to rise. This seemed more burdensome than reasonable for a punk. More likely, he wouldn't notice the useless suspenders hooked his boots. He'd catch on his heel, become entangled and fall over.

The clerks certainly didn't notice this oversight, so when nobody was looking, I tucked the suspenders up and over the boots. Problem solved.

Mental note: when I make these pants mine, I'll just avoid squatting.

On further investigation, I learned the trousers were dry-clean only, promising an expensive relationship with the garment. I guess this made sense if washing them would be like running a load of my mother's cutlery.

All these impossible extravagances and an inability to squat properly, coupled with a breathtaking price tag of two hundred and fifty dollars, made the pants prohibitively impractical. To a fifteen-year-old, they were perfect.

If they were mine, I would never take them off, except maybe to get them dry cleaned. Then I'd have to get a second pair, to wear while the other was at the cleaners. Even if it was going to take a small fortune, I was determined to find a way.

A small fortune, by the way, seemed a curious prerequisite to being a punk.

It seemed unlikely the clerks would be willing to hide their entire stock of those beauties until I'd gathered enough money to purchase the first pair. Of course, this meant there was only a thin window of time until one of my frienemies with enough cash to blow would discover them and buy a pair before me. Then *they* would be the first to wear my pants to school. Then everything would be *ruined*.

I had to act fast.

I could always try stealing them, but a recent arrest and short detention with the Lynnwood Police had sobered me from what might've been a promising future in shoplifting. My after-school job paid only twenty dollars a day. Even after two months of thrift and dedication I'd only managed to save fifty dollars. The pants would remain just beyond reach.

But this was not about a scarf. This was not something I could just let go and not think about, like a pair of sunglasses or gloves. The nagging would not subside until, finally, I decided to make them myself.

After all, this was about *pants*.

My sister Alissa, visiting from college, made the mistake of stopping by my room. On the floor I had splayed out a pair of my best pants like a little ritual sacrifice, but without the candles or chicken blood.

"What's all this?" she asked, bewildered.

"Nothing."

She entered cautiously as I was crouched over, doctoring apart the seams (with Mom's good paring knife) of what had been a faithful pair of polyester wranglers. Their fit was precise and satisfying from the seat to the cuffs. Overuse had worn a hole in the crotch: the kiss of death for even a timeless pair of duds. Even still, I didn't have the heart to just throw them away—I'm not a monster.

She stood there for a while, not saying anything, just taking it all in. The maroon polyester, dissected, front from back, waistline and pockets, arranged and meticulously laid out for measurements. I'd only been working on the pants for a couple days, and already the complexity, the immensity of the undertaking, had overcome my whole room.

In her brief absence, things had clearly taken a turn for the weird.

"These," I explained, "were my best pair of pants."

"Yes," she shuddered. "How could I forget?"

I showed her how I was saving every scrap and labeling them to use for a pattern. Actually, I was a little proud to have found such a useful end for my favorite pants. Their memory would live on and on.

"Super duper," she said, not understanding.

To illustrate, I showed her a couple pictures from my record collection, pictures of the Sex Pistols, Sham 69, Operation Ivy, Dead Kennedys, the Germs and Circle Jerks—her face went pallid.

"Those pants look like shit!"

"They're punk!" I said, clutching my records away from her. "That's part of the whole—*thing*."

She wasn't having any of it. She dragged me to the Alderwood Mall with the promise of an Orange Julius and at least one set of real clothes to wear, at least, while she was home. She was in college, after all, and she'd seen a lot in her time there. She knew how important it was to dress nice, to always present yourself the way you would at any job interview.

"If you look like you're homeless," she said to the windshield, driving a little too fast, "people are going to treat you like you're homeless."

We visited J. Crew and The Gap and JCPenney but not Mr. Rags since I'd just been arrested there. I even tried on a couple outfits, sulking out of various changing rooms, bristling against pleated khakis and tapered slacks, argyle sweater vests and pastel Polo shirts.

"See, there," she said, impressed. "You look so handsome!"

I was skeptical. To her mounting frustration, I turned down each item, until finally we had our little meltdown at a fountain by the food court.

"You want to look like shit?!" she was yelling, but not yelling. "Fine. I am *through*. You win."

Of course, by "you win," the implication was, "you lose." I lose on life. I lose respect from everyone. I lose out on a wealth of opportunity so impressive that, if I listened close, I could hear all those doors in my future, slamming shut.

In the middle of explaining how comfortable I was with my choices, some guy approached and politely tapped my sister on her shoulder.

"Excuse me, Miss?" he asked, smacking of spearmint gum.

He was dressed in a various assembly of all the clothes I'd just rejected, topped with crunchy hair, polished dress shoes and swirling with cologne. He had a gold pen and a clipboard.

"I have to ask, are you here looking for a job?"

"Ha," she said. "No, I'm visiting. Home from college."

"Well, I work here, and I'd like to offer you a job. You look exactly like the type of person we want working for us."

With that, they both turned and looked at me, beaming the way you would if the whole transaction was a set-up.

The project took months, a little snip here and a lot of stitching there, chasing after tiny country-shaped territories of fabric and keeping them all labeled and organized, all with an eye to the plaid, of course.

Plaid, it turns out, is a surprisingly tricky medium. Ensuring the pattern was even and running in the same direction was a task that required an obnoxious degree of strategy. Even the belt loops had to be sewn individually—something I'd never considered until then: how belt loops are made. While the pockets and the upper waistline were much more complex than I could have predicted, this was nothing compared to the crotch. Convincing the four corners of the crotch into the same neighborhood took no small amount of bullshitting and cigarettes. The union was bound by a messy network of unsightly, drunken stitches which, if they were unavoidable, were at least tucked away where the sun didn't shine.

So far, all this had been completed on a sewing machine that was, to be kind, a jalopy. It gobbled hungrily at the fabric, which was cheap and thin as cheesecloth. Often, the machine's feeder hogged the cloth in bunches under the presser foot until the needle seized, choking the bobbin in wads of thread and pant. Unraveling such a clog required the machine's complete disassembly, starting again and again, replacing the needle, walking the thread through its six-point guides and extricating and rewinding the bobbin and mounting it within the bobbin case, only to have the cloth bunch and trap again.

It took much longer than necessary to conclude I was spending far more time working on the sewing machine than on the pants.

I finally abandoned the smoldering heap, resuming the massive project by hand, my fingertips blistered and raw with measuring and cutting and pinning and endless stitching under the flickering neon lights of my bedroom.

It was late at night when I put the finishing touches to the pants. Their only resemblance to the floor-modeled inspiration: they were both pants, both plaid. Mine had no buckles or drapery, no pocketless zippers or useless tangle of mock suspenders. Their squat quotient, I am happy to report, was bonafide.

Even though I doubled up the fabric, the pants were still incredibly thin. I took them out for a test walk, even the wind from a swishing stride flowed through the legs as if through a screen door.

But they looked so damn good!

I stayed up through the night, playing records and modeling them this way and that in my floor-length mirror, catching the dangerously handsome reflection to ask, "Who's that?" I tried a variety of different accessories with the pants, but really they could've looked smashing with any old thing. I finally decided to pair them with a ratty blazer, similarly decorated with safety-pinned patches and a bouquet of buttons on the lapel. For the pièce de résistance, a pair of steel-toed, oxblood saddle shoes.

I was ready for school.

At least I had the forethought to bring a needle and an extra spool of thread because, on the bus, a public transit line, one of the cuffs began inching its way loose. I got some pretty strange looks, sewing that shut, when I noticed a thigh seam was actually pulling right through the thin fabric. The widening gap ran from the inside knee almost up to the crotch, leaving a long ragged tassel. Repairing such a wound required additional measures, none of which were available at school.

I could see the building, less than a quarter mile down the hill from the bus stop. All I had to do was make it to school, so I could be seen, so I could be the first one to show up in a rad pair of plaid pants.

Plaid pants! Who would've thought of such a thing?

Me, that's who. Boom.

My waistline curiously loosening, I pressed on through the parking lot.

The pants got a lot of looks. I certainly turned a lot of heads, not because I was suddenly the foremost fashionista on campus. More likely because, in the distance between the bus stop and the wide doors of the main entrance, just yards away now, the pants had somehow dissolved to a wad of swaddling, which I desperately clutched around my waist.

Our new vice-principal, Mr. Torres, who'd likely been warned about me by the outgoing vice-principal, rushed out to greet me before I could even reach the door. He made a formidable blockade, holding out both hands saying "Nope. Nope. Nope. Noooooooo."

He caught me by the shoulders.

"Go home, Barber. When you come back, tardy, you'll need to be wearing pants."

He stepped back to get a good look at my bare thighs, my knocking knees and the deep red, steel-toe saddle shoes which now looked remarkably like clown shoes.

"I mean, *come on.*"

I gathered my loin rags and moped back to the bus stop at the top of the hill.

The bus driver didn't say anything, but opened the door with a long, exaggerated *"kids today."* His bus took me to the Lynnwood park-n-ride and the busy crowds of morning commuters to wait for my transfer. The commuters all seemed delighted to be greeted by this bit of comedy on their way to work. In this crowd of people, I waited for my bus, pretending nothing was out of the ordinary about clutching a pile of rags around my bare, shivering thighs.

The Tenants

I packed up the house and left a mint on the kitchen counter.

The mint, I thought, would be a comforting touch for the coming tenants as they explored their new home. I swept the floors, then mopped the floors on my hands and knees. There was no hint of dust on the windowsills. The bathrooms glistened with a punch of bleach and Windex: a combination both toxic and surgically clean.

I saved a last cup of coffee for one last relax in the breakfast nook, to enjoy alone its candied scent of naked cedar and bacon, before indulging in one last tour—committing to memories—the hallway, the kitchen and circular downstairs plan. The house was two stories, with a wide, warming entry. A bare wood, block-and-rung banister, polished in the odd places frequently grasped or caressed on the way up or down a staircase that creaked low and oaky.

How the house echoed!

With no furniture, or carpets or pictures on the walls, or the constant mess on the floor, even the light "poc" of an easy footstep rang in whispers from the cold bare rooms and shuttered into woody closets. It was in these mockingly well-lit, caramel hallways and cozy alcoves where our marriage had, at long last, sputtered to a glottal stop.

I waited for too long, lingering in a room upstairs. It was a bedroom I had swept and scrubbed immaculately clean but ultimately failed to remove its soaked-in history—the many things I'd rather forget.

Three days I spent in this room, nursing my then wife back to health.

She'd just lost the pregnancy with her coworker and I stayed there with her, by her bedside, dumbstruck by this tragedy and other tragedies, including the sudden death of my brother, which, timing impeccable, occurred on the very same day I confronted her about the affair.

After that calm, balmy morning in July, my three days as caretaker ended precisely at 5:30 in the morning when she was well enough to eat again, and to walk on her own. It might seem heartless, but I had her in the car that very instant.

A friend of hers said she could stay with her until she was able to find an apartment. I drove her there, but when we arrived, her friend was not home, or was not yet awake. I left her there anyway with her bags and a lamp. We could sort out the DVDs later.

When I was done with her, it was also clear I was done with most everything else.

I closed the bedroom door. The house was a shell of walls, pressing in. It squeezed until, no matter how I might have clung to that polished banister, I popped right out the front door.

Dale Kendrick:
Janitor/Rogue Assassin

Throngs of sunburnt meanderthals and their feral, sticky-face children flocked from the suburbs to descend on the science museum like a plague of locusts. The museum opened at 9:00 a.m., which was clearly posted in several locations. In spite of this, the crowds, eager for their children to destroy something besides the living room, started banging on the doors at 8:30.

I pointed to my watch and shrugged a mock apology which, of course, had an effect similar to flicking an aquarium full of army ants. Maybe it was petty, enjoying their reaction—the bared-teeth indignation as they were made to wait outside—but it was one of the few luxuries of a customer service supervisor.

I finally opened the doors at 9:02.

Instantly, the lobby was a clog of double-wide, all-terrain strollers and children who'd been promised ice cream and candy and popcorn and hot dogs. Once they were finally fed, most of the food was dumped on the ground and mashed under their sneakers. What they did manage to stuff in their maw was wolfed down so quickly it usually came right back up again, most often in a carpeted area or the upholstered seats of the motion simulator or the Imax theater.

Through it all, Dale Kendrick steered his janitor's cart, always with a smile and a pair of latex gloves. I've never seen him *not* smiling. He was always so peaceful, passing gracefully, almost absurdly polite through this fog of war.

I loved Dale and always looked forward to our conversations. He had a sturdy handshake and was thoughtful enough to remove his latex glove before our usual greeting. He was always eager for my daily horror stories from the front desk, which he repaid with the far more interesting tales from the janitor's rounds. Once he fished half a cadaver, just a woman's torso really, out of the Willamette River, coaxing it ashore with a broomstick.

"Hey! Hey! Hey!" he said, shaking my hand vigorously. "What tales from the front desk?"

Finally I said, "Dale, man. What's your secret?"

"What do you mean?"

"I mean, you look like a million bucks! With all these people—these horrible, awful people—"

He demurred, "Oh poo, this is the best job on earth!"

Just then, the lobby was split by a blood curdling scream: a toddler, red faced and howling at another toddler who was barfing down his front. Their parents or guardians, presumably, ignored them both, continued to chat unperturbed, nearby.

"I'll tell you my secret," said Dale, leaning in, looking left and right, almost whispering, "I am Shadrak Obsidian, leader of the world's most feared clan of murderous assassins for hire." He gave a little wink and a curtsy, "At your service."

He spun a spray bottle from a side holster, "Duty calls!"

After the six o'clock closing announcement, it usually took the security and janitors an additional thirty minutes to locate and remove the lingering visitors from various hiding places. Dale discovered a couple upstairs in the Earth Science Hall trying the locked doors to the back hallways and administrative offices.

Every now and then, somebody slipped in through a keyhole. They're usually found late at night wandering the hallways. Everyone I've caught sneaking around plead the same excuse: "I can't find my way out!" as if they'd managed to overlook every exit sign, every door leading outside.

Dale escorted the couple from the darkened, locked halls. He saw them to the door, returning to the front desk, shaking his head the whole way.

"They said," said Dale. "They were looking for a way out."

"A way out of what?" I asked. "Their pants?"

He took off a latex glove to give me a high five.

"Dale, what's this business about Shadrak—"

"Shhhh!" he said, waving his hands at me. He pointed over my shoulder.

The front lobby was filling with Russians: our regulars on Friday and Saturday nights.

"Don't worry about them. They don't even speak English."

"They don't speak English?"

"Well, some do. Barely."

"But they're here to see an Imax movie?"

I told Dale the Russians all belong to one of the ultra con-servative mega-churches on 82nd. Baptists I think. They came in large groups, our museum being one of the few places the boys and girls are allowed to congregate outside of the church. It didn't matter the movies were in English, and that *Dolphins*, *Antarctica* and *The Living Sea* aren't exactly date-movie material.

"Let's just say," I said, "none of them are here to actually watch the movie."

Jenny, a new customer service representative butted in, "How do you know they're Russians? Isn't that racist?"

I had to think about that for a second. The crowd assem-bled by the front doors gathered in separate groups—boys and girls. The boys all looked like mafioso brats in shiny Armani suits with huge shoulder pads, a tie being their only variation. The girls all wore the same short, sparkly prom cast-offs, sti-letto heels and identical hairdos, glittered and sprayed into place with a modest pompadour. They'd all been marinated in cologne and perfume.

"No," I said.

"Wow," said Jenny with high, judging eyebrows. "I just think it's a little presumptuous of you is all."

I pointed behind her. "Look sharp, Jenny."

The Russians sent two representatives, boy negotiators, who approached the front desk. One asked Jenny with a thick, vampire accent, "How much Omnimax movie?"

Dale was just loving this whole interaction.

"See?" I told him. "Harmless. Now, tell me about this Shadrak—"

"Shhhshshsh!!!" he lit again. Looking left, right, he pointed to a dark corner. "Meet me over there. I'll tell you everything."

I left Jenny to haggle with the Russians and found Dale, mousing around in a shady corner by the Turbine Hall.

"What I'm about to tell you," he hushed. "You can't tell anybody else. Ever."

"I promise," I lied.

Dale wasn't kidding around when he said he was the leader of the world's most feared clan of assassins and killers. Shadrak Obsidian was Dale Kendrick's avatar in a popular online RPG.

"Stop there," I said. "I'm already lost."

I was embarrassed to not have guessed that RPG stood for role playing game. His RPG was a warcraft something-or-other: an immeasurably complex universe of thieves, murderers, warring tribes and on and on. The game has no end. Instead it's a long history of intrigues and conquests, defeats and victories all puppeted continuously by ordinary people like Dale Kendrick.

"It's going on right now!" he said.

"What, you're playing right now?"

"Well, Shadrak is resting because I'm here, at work. He's probably snoozing in the bunker with the rest of the clan. We've got a couple sentinels out to watch the compound."

"Sentinels? You mean, people log on to the game to keep a look out? That's all they do?"

Jenny left the front desk, walking quickly over to us. The

two Russians remained at her register, arguing quietly. Dale saw her approaching and seamlessly joked, "—and that's why I'll never eat Chinese food again!"

Jenny urged, "They want to know how much the movie is."

"I know," I said. "Did you point out the price board above your head?"

She crossed her arms and scowled at me, sour at my obvious suggestion. The Russians eyed our huddle suspiciously.

"*Of course* I pointed out the prices. They won't pay more than four dollars a person."

"Yes well, the price is ten dollars." I gave Jenny a reassuring tap on her shoulder. "Go get 'em tiger!"

When Jenny was a safe distance away, returning to the Russians who were already raising their voices, Dale continued.

"Aside from just standing guard, sentinels also do the dishes and clean the bunkhouse. Normally while we're out on a raid or something."

I was having a visibly difficult time wrapping my mind around Dale's RPG. I had enough real-life dishes of my own and couldn't imagine unwinding by doing someone else's digital dishes.

Dale shrugged, "Just like anywhere, you've got to start somewhere. It takes a lot of dishes, a lot of floors swept to work your way up to a clan's warrior status. Unless," Dale sneered, "you're one of those rich kids who buys your way in."

It was fascinating to watch Dale peel back the social matrix that governed Shadrak's world. How Dale first earned his fortune in gold and status washing his fair share of dishes and sweeping countless floors free of its digital dust. Then, as a warrior, he hacked and maimed and invaded his way to the top, only to be greeted there by some fifteen-year-old kid who used his dad's credit card to buy a Warrior's Elite passcode on a users forum. Dale had no respect for line cutters and took a special pleasure in hunting them down, violently closing their accounts and sending them back to the end of the line.

Nothing drove Dale crazy like the cheats, the Lag Cappers, Flyhackers and Wintraders and all the others the Blizz refused to do anything about. Blizz, or the Blizzard, referred to Blizzard Entertainment, the developers of the game. They were generally known as the faceless overlords that established and enforced the rules. To see Dale talk about the cheats, the arbitrary and mystifying ambivalence of the Blizz, was unsettling. His constant smile and glittering eyes drained to a slack of gravity. His face and shoulders melted and tensed, shuddering to recall the injustices he suffered at the hands of this cruel universe.

In spite of all this, Dale managed to keep his head up, and Shadrak's head attached to his shoulders. He sallied forth, chopping up and killing his opponents and stealing their gold until Shadrak Obsidian became one of the most powerful icons in contemporary gaming.

"—and that's," Dale shouted suddenly, "*the last* time I'll ever eat Mexican food!"

Jenny was standing next to me, "They want to talk to you."

"Who?" I feigned.

"The Russians! Of course."

"Whoa whoa whoa!" I scoffed. "How do you know they're Russian?"

Keeping his house of assassins in order took much of his time outside of work. There was a lot of infighting and grumbling among his ranks. The politics of keeping alpha, and holding his small army in line took most of the time he had available to play. He was rarely able to get out there and raise hell.

He'd drop by the front desk to keep me posted. "I finally killed the head of House Orrix!" he'd say. Or "We enslaved over half the Trybuald Clan, decapitated the rest and took all their gold!"

"Whoa!" I said, having no idea what he was talking about. "*All* their gold? That's nuts!" Slowly, I was able to piece together the maneuvers, the strategy that bound the clans and set rivalries.

Most of his clan was scattered around the world. It was a sprawling network. Players of all levels working in every time zone. So it was likely someone in his clan was always up to something while the other avatars were logged off. This, too, explained why he was so secretive about Shadrak Obsidian.

He told me once, "There's spies everywhere. Could even be that one, up there."

I looked to the line winding from the registers at the front desk.

"Who?"

"That one, there."

I looked to where Dale was nodding, to a woman arguing with one of our cashiers about the validity of a coupon that expired seven years ago. Two of her five kids wore only sagging diapers and she was ignoring the Journey ring tone coming from her sweaty bra.

"I dunno, Dale."

"No," he said. "*The boy.*"

Sure enough, behind this spectacle was a pimply face kid in a Monster Energy drink shirt, boring directly at Dale with unflinching, knowing eyes.

He shrugged, "Bring it kiddo. You're dead meat, all of you pipsqueaks."

Some of his clan lived here in Portland. He saw them sometimes at the grocery store. Sometimes, they'd even come into the museum with their families, and while they were polite, they never spoke. At the most, they'd offer a quick nod and move on.

"It's a different world in there. You're a different person. And never the two shall meet."

One night, Dale pushed his cart aimlessly by the front desk. He looked right past me, maybe even talking to himself. Half his shirt was untucked and his ponytail had come undone. He was wearing only one latex glove.

I called out, but he didn't hear me as he sailed past the front desk, muttering.

When I caught up to him later, he was definitely talking to himself, shaking his head. I called out again and he squinted my way, disoriented, trying to recognize me. When I came closer, he shifted, cornered and nervous, throwing some serious shade.

"You okay? Dale?"

He finally recognized me, but without relief.

"Heavy lies the crown—" he said.

"Dale. What is going on?"

"Things are... I might need to leave early tonight. Well, I'll get all the trashes and vacuum, sure. Then I've got to get back home. I've got something I need to—" He trailed off.

"Is there trouble? Online?"

"Huh? What?!" he looked up, suddenly leery. "Why do you ask?"

"You look—" I pointed to his naked hand. "Out of sorts. Is Shadrak in trouble?"

"Oh, yeah, ha ha," he slid his hand into another latex glove. "Shadrak's in a heap of trouble, bro."

The night before, Shadrak Obsidian and the clan of assassins he lorded over were visited by a cloaked stranger in a heavy storm.

"Wait, there's storms in there?"

"Oh, yeah, there's weather just like outside. Some of our finest battles were won because we caught so-and-so off guard in the middle of a cold snap. Anyway, we were all inside for the night, mostly plotting and making dinner—"

I was still having difficulty grappling with a game that involved the daily tedium of making dinner.

"—when all of a sudden, there was a pounding on our door."

Dale told everyone to stand down, but some asshole playing from Latvia, his avatar's name is Goregall or something, he went and opened the door anyway. The door creaked open to a downpour and lightning outlining a hulking figure in the doorway. Either he'd slipped past the sentinels, or he killed them all. Anyway, there he was, and he raised a finger, pointing to Shadrak.

"BEWARE!" said Dale with a mock wheeze, grabbing my

shoulder. "There is a traitor in your house!"

Of course, he killed him right away, but the dark stranger managed to rasp a warning past Shadrak's steely grip.

"It's one of youuuuuuuu," said Dale. His eyes were huge, dancing and crazy, then breaking off, looking over my shoulder, darting left and right. He was pouring sweat.

"Dale, it's probably nothing to worry about," I said. "Isn't this a thing you told me about? Just some rogue centurion from a rival house, a bit of throwaway code they conjured to poison your house."

"Even if that's the case, it's working, bro. It's got everyone helluh spooked. They're all threatening a mutiny. I mean, you gotta remember, the number of hours some of these guys put into their avatars... it's not just a video game." He gripped my shoulder tighter. "This is our *lives* we're talking about."

"Jeez Dale," I said. "What are you going to do?"

"Well, you gotta lock that down is what! Purge the ranks."

Evenings after it closed, the museum was an eerie, haunted place to wander. There's something unnatural and creepy about a place designed to accommodate and entertain a massive bustle of people when it's closed, empty and dark and still. The next time I saw Dale, he looked like a ghost, haunting one of the hollow halls.

He was standing alone, in the long hall with wide windows that looked out on the night like a black aquarium. He was always very pale, but now his skin looked almost blue in the moonlight, like wet putty. His shirt was untucked. His cart was nowhere to be seen, and he'd been dragging a bag of trash behind him. He was looking out at the long night, at the river and the thin curl of moon setting behind the dark apron of the looming west hills.

"Dale?"

He saw my reflection in the window but didn't turn. He was muttering again, worrying at the hem of the garbage bag.

I joined him at the window.

"Pretty night." I sounded so stupid.

"Well," he finally said, "I did it. I said I was going to purge the ranks…"

On the verge of tears, he told me how he tried to consolidate Shadrak's power but it was already too late. His men began to turn on each other. From grudges materialized insinuations, which grew to accusations, which turned to scuffles until someone lost an ear.

That was two nights ago.

Dale was in his kitchen, making some mac and cheese when his computer and his phone both started going bonkers.

He logged in and everyone was standing around and there was this avatar screaming bloody about his ear. It was sliced clean off, and missing. They bandaged him up, but the missing ear drove a spike through the house. Everybody agreed to log off for a day and cool their heads.

As it stood, Dale's house was fractured.

"This slimy, spineless simp, Timmy. I think he's a line cook at La Casa Ralph. He was making a big show about breaking away and leading his own house. You can't have that. Not to keep the order."

Dale went back to the moon. His face was sunken. Had he

lost weight?

"Is Timmy the traitor?"

"Maybe. Anyway, it doesn't matter now. I killed them all."

"You what?!"

"I killed them all. Thirty-two warriors. Fine men, all of them. But they had to go. It's the only way to be certain."

It was a hell of a fight of course. Now everyone was vowing revenge. Shadrak was an expert warrior with enough gold and plunder to begin an empire, but he was an outcast now, hunted. The Blizz didn't shut down his account, but he was blacklisted from anyone who might trade with him. The best chance he had was to bury what he could, which would be a fraction of his winnings, and disappear. For certain nobody would be so polite as to give Dale so much as a nod in the grocery store, or the museum.

"Everything is lost!" he said to the windows. "*Lost.*"

"Look on the bright side," I tried. "At least you found out who the spy was."

"Nope. Never found out who it was remember? I killed everybody."

"No, I mean, the traitor was Shadrak Obsidian."

"What?"

"Shadrak killed everyone didn't he? Didn't you? He's the only one left so he must've been the traitor."

"No, but, *I'm* Shad—" and then Dale snapped away from the black hills, mouth open, stammering. "Oh my god," he said, pushing the trash bag in my hands. "Oh my god I need to go."

"'Oh my god' what? Dale! Where are you—"

"I need to go home. *Right now.*"

145

He stripped off his latex gloves and dropped them in the trash. He smoothed back his ponytail and whipped it into a band then, tucking in his shirt, ran full tilt to the parking lot.

Happy Thanksgiving!

Only three days as a busboy at the Lynnwood Red Robin and I was already looking for a new job. It's not that I was above the work of a busboy. It was good, hard work that paid reasonably well. With the right attitude, your head down and mouth shut, the work could actually pass quickly.

As a busboy, I was not the lowest on the totem pole. That was the dishwashers who were either on a work release from some correctional institution or on a tightly regulated stay from Mexico. Then came the kitchen staff and their intricate subcategories of merit. Then the bus staff, food expediters and waiters in training. Finally, there was the wait staff, who were basically royalty, having scrambled up this disheartening gauntlet. They'd been worked like dogs, long and hard, to secure the coveted positions at the very tippy-top of the restaurant's social pyramid. Their rank was hard won and shamelessly flaunted.

With the rewards of their royal status came a notorious drowsy spell capable of derailing a job from a means to an end to an end-all. Waiters abandoned their schooling mid-degree. Those who were saving for amazing travel plans saw their earnings somehow morph into rent and bills. For many, becoming a waiter at the Red Robin was reaching a summit, and they would ride it out for as long as possible. Hopefully it was not their only peak, but their comfortable, enviable rank and the social currency it paid wove a tender trap.

My manager Linda reminded me often, "Work long enough, and hard enough, and someday you too may become one of our waiters."

Whether this was a promise or a threat was hard to discern.

Mind you, all this played out in a burger emporium whose whole schtick was the carnival gayety of happy times and gourmet burgers presented by a team of campy cartoon bird mascots.

Here the waiters didn't just offer a polite "happy birthday." They gathered a crowd, took a chair, and climbed up on the chair to shout and clap out the "Birthday Song" to anyone who couldn't scramble away fast enough. The menus were 25.5 inches long by 14 inches wide and listed a selection of entrees presumably named after the rides at Disneyland.

Whisky River Barbecue Burger.

Red's Nantucket Seafood Scatter.

Mountain High Mudd Pie.

What did I want with a job like this? To be swept up in this grim procession of candy-ass suck-ups who openly ached and pined for their own claustrophobic spot at the top? This was, small time. This wasn't for me. I'd always imagined I would go out there and make a difference. I would do good, amazing things and eventually end up on the cover of *National Geographic*, humble but earnest, maybe cupping a clump of rich earth, the root ball of a redwood sapling.

Little did I know how soon I would get my big break.

It was the night before Thanksgiving and I was a twenty-year-old busboy.

Half through the evening rush, I ordered a burger for dinner with extra steak fries. To wait for my food, I stepped out to the garbage dock and was just about to light a cigarette when I heard a faint whimpering, soft and sniffling, coming from behind the dumpsters. I followed the sound, around the corner. Hiding next to the dumpster was a little girl. She saw me and frightened back, crying harder.

I put the cigarettes away.

She was clutching one of our red-checked food wrappers, someone's half eaten burger and fries. When I came closer, she dropped the food and wedged herself further back, between rancid barrels of fry grease.

"Hey—" I said, low. "Hey, are you okay?"

She shook her head.

"Are you hungry?"

She shook her head again.

"Where are your parents? Are you lost?"

"I lost—" she said.

I came a step closer.

"Are your parents around?"

She nodded, pointing to the grease-slick stairs leading up and around the back of the dumpster where I could hear rustling and voices coming from inside the dumpster. She picked up another package of food from a torn bag, opened it and started poking around inside.

I climbed the stairs slowly and spied over the edge of the dumpster.

A man was waist deep in torn black bags, spilling several days of food waste. A woman was in there with him, but they didn't look up. They'd torn through almost all the bags in the dumpster and were looking through each wadded-up pouch of red-checked parchment.

Before they saw me, I backed away from the filthy edge of the bin, back down the stairs. The little girl didn't look up, just kept picking through another cold pile of food and sobbing quietly.

In the break room, a gathering of bussers and waitresses were spending their lunch break captivated by Guy Jessie, our bobblehead bartender with a molester moustache. He was a popped-collar hotshot, trash talking a group of guys who'd stiffed him on a huge tab. He was convinced they were Mexican.

I interrupted his rant, "Did you guys see that family? Out on our loading dock?"

Guy still had his hands in the air, mid-illustration. He scoffed, shocked I'd had the gall to interrupt his story.

"There was a little girl, and her parents were—"

"*So, what?*" said Guy. His face, squinched-up like a ferret. "Newbie."

Some of the waitresses giggled.

"They were inside the dumpster!" I said. "Her dad, maybe he was up to his waist in food and trash."

Guy turned to Nancy, a cocktail waitress. Everyone knew they were sleeping together even though Guy was dating one of the hostesses and Nancy was engaged to one of the waiters. He flipped a tuft of his thick, luxurious hair and said, "Maybe you should just mind your own business?"

Nancy laughed and said, "Yeah, like, they're trying to enjoy a nice Thanksgiving dinner."

Guy and Nancy thought this was super hilarious. They laughed and laughed, pawing at each other aggressively.

"That's not funny," I said.

Guy spritzed his fingers at me. "Oooohhhh. The newbie doesn't think I'm funny?!"

"You know what?" I said. "I'm going to have my dinner wrapped up. Yeah! And I'm going to give it to them."

He swatted the air. "Well, *lah-dee-dah*."

"No," said another waitress. "He's right. I'm going to give them my salad."

"Stacy. You can not be serious," said Nancy.

Trevor, another busser, joined in, "I'm going to give them my burger! *And* my fries!"

Three against two!

Guy put up his hands, "Fuck off anyway. Do-gooders are full of shit."

Together, Trevor, Stacy and I, would go hungry for the night. Together, we had the line cooks wrap our dinners to-go with an extra serving of steak fries and plenty of condiments. One of the line cooks wanted to know what was up, and when I told her about the family, she was so excited she threw in a Tango Mango Tiki Chicken Salad with almost a whole loaf of Garlic Naughties. I wrote on their bag with a big, thick pen— "HAPPY THANKSGIVING!" with a smiley face and sealed the steaming bag shut.

It must have been fifteen pounds of food in there.

Outside, on the loading dock, the little girl was still there, still crying in a larger pile of wrappers.

"Hey," I whispered. "Hey girl. C'mere." I waved her over.

She looked to the dumpster.

"It's okay. C'mere. Quiet."

She put down the wrapper and came over to me and Stacy and Trevor, but stopped just beyond a reach, sniffling.

I offered the huge bag of hot food on a milk crate between us. I told the girl Thanksgiving was my favorite holiday, which it was. I told her, I hoped she and her family had a happy Thanksgiving, as much as possible. I said I hoped she would be okay and that they'd find somewhere warm to spend the holidays.

Stacy even whispered, "God bless you, little one!"

Backing away from the girl, we shut the door behind us.

Lunch break was over, Guy and Kathy were making out by the time clock.

"Hey Lancelot," said Guy, lipstick smeared. "Did you save a life tonight, Lancelot?"

I punched in my employee code. I gathered a bleach rag and a rotten bus bin and, chin up, returned to the restaurant floor.

By midnight, most the staff was out in the parking lot, binge drinking and waiting for the late crew to clock off and drive them to wherever the party was.

I finished my side work and finally clocked off as well, tagging along with the line cooks who needed help picking up beer. Outside, a crowd was shuffling around Guy Jessie's hot IROC-Z, but nobody was cheering or shouting as usual.

There was the little girl, standing with them. Her parents were there too. They were caked in food and sauce, the three of them.

The little girl was still choking on wet sobs, holding one of our white to-go boxes. Her mother looked at her feet, or looked away. The man, presumably her father, was shouting and shaking the bag of food at Guy Jessie who was draped over his pathetic muscle car, peeling with laughter. Guy nudged this furious man with a longneck bottle of beer and said something, pointing me out.

"Hey-O! Here's Lancelot now, asshole."

The man came at me, steering the little girl in front of him. His lips peeled back, gleaning a handful of sour teeth.

"You!" he yelled. "Yeah, YOU!"

The line cooks, the rest of the group, backed away from me.

"You think we need this? This— *shit*?"

His breath was a fume of red onion and heavy alcohol. He held up the bag for me to see.

"HAPPY THANKSGIVING!"

He tore the bag in two, slopping the still-hot mess at my feet and kicking the food at me.

"You think this is funny? You want us to have a happy

Thanksgiving? Is that right?"

I braced, ready for a punch to the mouth, for a fight, but nothing came. He just kicked the food around and kept shouting insults and names and drunk-ass nonsense, still holding onto the little girl's hand. When that got old, he let her go and spat at my feet and turned and steamed away, leaving the little girl and me there on the sidewalk.

The bag read, "HAPPY TH" and "ANKSGIVING!" and had been stomped into the wet pavement.

The girl, still holding a white to-go box, opened the small box and held it out for me to see.

I took a peek inside the box.

Inside was a small pink blob. I craned in closer to get a better look at the tiny pink gnarl of wire and plastic.

"I lost—I threw it away," she sniffled. "My only retainer."

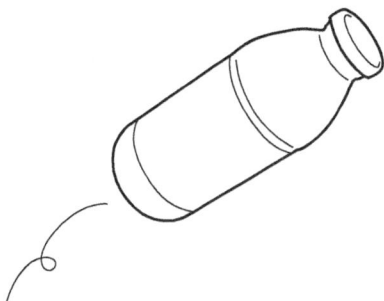

Paris, France.
Lynnwood, Washington.

That summer I was on exchange with Jerome, who was also thirteen years old. He lived just south of Paris.

Paris was unlike anything. France! Everything you've heard about the wonderful country, there to just—walk around, soak it up.

Jerome's family kindly put me up in the oldest brother's room (a camp counselor, he was away for the summer). It was too hot to sleep with the covers on and there were far too many mosquitoes to sleep without covers. Their tiny hum rang in my ears. I'd swat and slap them away, but moments later the brave pests would light again and again until, pockmarked with fiery bumps, I turned on the light and rolled up a copy of *Les Inrockuptibles*.

I worked until late at night, deliriously jet lagged and,

tracking the tiny mosquitoes by their telltale buzz, smashing them with the magazine. Eventually I killed them all and the room was silent.

Riddled with itch, I fell asleep hard and didn't wake up until Jerome's mother opened the shades late the next morning, almost noon. She was yelling French, screaming at me and pointing around the room like a madwoman.

Blinking awake, I could finally see what she was pointing at: a grim horror scene, decorated by dark smears and splatters of my blood caked with a mash of legs and wings, the gored copy of *Les Inrockuptibles* by the bedside. We worked through lunch, for hours, scrubbing at the uncleanable eggshell of the plaster walls, my grumpy hostess grumbling unknowns as we scrubbed and scrubbed.

For the month I stayed with his family, we took the train to the city as much as possible. I had my first souvlaki. We made a dizzying tour of food and museums, cathedrals and alleys. As my guide, Jerome noted once, almost as an afterthought, a residence we were walking past used to be Victor Hugo's. We took a weeklong trip to the Normandy coast, to the beaches American and Allied forces stormed on D-day.

I received my first kiss, from an English girl. She put her tongue down my throat right in front of her parents.

We spent a day at Mont St-Michel, saw the Château du Caen and the Bayeux Tapestry. These things were older than anything I'd seen. I certainly didn't understand them, or their place in the world, but I was forever changed by the encounter.

The following month, Jerome came to stay with us, in our home in Lynnwood, Washington. We had a Costco and the Alderwood Mall and some parks. To a visitor or passerby, Lynnwood was most effectively introduced by the Black Angus Steakhouse next to the I-5 off-ramp. The restaurant's massive, well-lit sign proudly called to the north and southbound travelers: *Black Angus*, except for the "g," perhaps the most important letter on that sign, which fizzled out and remained unrepaired for several years.

It was late at night when we peeled off the freeway toward our home, the last leg in Jerome's very long trip. His eyes were bleary but nailed to that sign, lips mulling an unsure translation. Finally he asked, "What is this: *Black Anus*?"

Jerome was eager to know: what was there to do in Lynnwood?

"There's the 7-Eleven," I said confidently. "And Lyndale Park. We go there sometimes to ride bikes."

"We cannot go to Seattle? I would like to see more of this."

I said we could but warned him of our public transportation system, how it was not really transportation. It was more of a cruel joke, its humor wouldn't translate well into French. Its humor didn't translate well into English, for that matter.

As this sunk in, Jerome seemed cagey, almost panicking.

He warbled, "I see. Okay."

Maybe he suspected this whole exchange was an elaborate American prank.

I suggested, "If you want to do something fun, sometimes, late at night, we sneak out and go to the 7-Eleven and play video games and eat candy."

"The little market down the street?" said Jerome, puzzled.

"That's the one," I said. "We'll have to avoid the police

157

because there's a curfew. But we usually walk there and back. It's cool."

Jerome, who at this point looked like he would've settled for cable television, seemed to rise at this slightly naughty prospect.

He said, "Okay. I will try this."

At one in the morning, we slipped out a window. I was first, then Jerome, and then my brother Patrick slid the window shut behind him. We tiptoed across the lawn to the street, then beyond our cul de sac until we were free. We were free but on the lookout for police. Every pair of headlights in the distance might be a cop who could catch us and return us home. It was all so exciting!

Jerome did not seem impressed.

He was similarly downcast when we rounded the corner strip mall to the 7-Eleven.

"There she is," I said.

"'Open twenty-four hours,'" read Jerome. "Why is this? There is nobody."

"Except us," said Patrick. "We're here. Let's have some fun."

"If you say so."

We pushed open the doors, blinking at the incredible neon light.

Janice, the 7-Eleven night clerk, folded her newspaper. She cooed, "Good evening boys."

I loved Janice. She was a Lynnwood institution, unapologetic and scandalous. She was incredibly elegant, even at one thirty in the morning. It was appropriate we should take Jerome to meet her. We told her Jerome was from France and she did a little shimmy, "Ooh la-la!"

They shook hands. The gold chains dangling from the her horn-rimmed glasses bounced and jiggled with the greeting. Her hair, a perfectly coiffed red swoop with blond streaks, did not move.

She broke a five into quarters, telling Jerome why she worked the night shift.

"My husband, Leonard, snores. So if I have to stay awake through the night, I might as well get paid to read the paper."

She was always eager to stop whatever she was doing and talk and talk. She would tell us all about the nightcrawlers who came in, high or drunk or in a crazy hurry for a pack of condoms. Tonight she left us to our video games. Almost immediately we'd spent all our quarters.

"You boys!" said Janice. "You need to learn how to stretch five bucks. Video games? Poof! When you meet a nice girl, you'll need a lot more than five bucks. But then, you'll need to know more than just video games. Am I right?"

I said, "Okay."

As we made our way back outside, Janice called, "Listen to your friend Jerome! The French—even the boys might teach you about girls."

Jerome was smitten, blushing hard as we stepped out to the sultry summer night.

"She was nice!" he said. "What is there now?"

"That's about it," I shrugged. "Back home."

"Lynnwood sucks," said Patrick. "There's nothing to do. And the people—" he jerked a thumb back at Janice buried in her newspaper.

"Shut up," I said. "I love Janice."

Patrick scoffed, "She's works the graveyard at a 7-Eleven—"

Just then, a group of three older boys, high schoolers, rounded the corner to the parking lot. The one with a letterman's jacket said something low and pointed at us. We hurried to get around them, but they stepped in front of us.

"Hey kids! What's up kids?" said Letterman, edging in menacingly. He wrapped an arm around my shoulder. "It's a nice night, eh? Nice night for a stroll? You guys out for a walk? Just—going on a walk?"

I didn't say anything. Jerome and Patrick froze.

I tried twisting loose of the arm but he locked tight, wringing the creaking leather arm of his jacket around my neck.

There was the familiar, faraway ding of the 7-Eleven door. Janice yelled, "Hey! You kids knock it off!"

One of them shouted, "Aw, it's okay lady. We're just having a little fun."

"*Let them go!*"

Letterman shouted, "Man! Fuck you, lady!"

Janice shut and locked the door and took up the phone.

The third boy said, "Dude, that's Janice. Come on Chad, knock it off—"

"Shut up Jason!" hissed another boy. "Get 'em Chad. Fuck him up!"

The parking lot was empty. There were no cars, only the sound of our shoes scuffing the pavement.

"I'll tell you what," said Chad. "I'm going to fuck you up now, and there isn't anything you can do about it."

He waited for this to sink in.

"Boys!" shouted Jerome. "Stop this! Stupid nonsense!"

Letterman was dislodged by the French accent. He dropped his grasp. His mouth hung open, wheels spinning as he stammered to regroup.

Jason pulled him away, "Come *on* Chad! Leave it."

The other boy threw up his hands and left, "Bo-ring!"

Chad pointed at me, said to Jerome, "Tell your faggot friend to watch his ass! Or, I'll... kick his ass!"

He pulled a punch and I flinched. He thought that was funny and did it again. I put up my hands, like swatting a mosquito.

Letterman pushed me back. "You're lucky," he said, backing away. "I'm not in the mood to beat your ass anyway. Guys! Hey, wait up guys!"

He ran after his friends who'd continued to the 7-Eleven.

We stood there, the three of us heaving for air, tiny fists clenched. We watched them joking and shouting across the parking lot. My ears and eyes burned. I was fixed on a glass bottle, ahead of me on the ground. It was a couple feet away, and empty. And then it was in my hand. And then it was sailing through the air, in a long graceful arc, toward the three boys.

For a sickening moment it looked like the heavy bottle would land right on one of their heads. But it dove between them and shattered, glass exploding everywhere.

"Fuck you!" I yelled. "Motherfuckerrrrrrs!"

They were already sprinting at us, full tilt.

We turned and ran.

We ran as fast as we could, with their heavy barking furious and gaining quick behind us.

"Here!" I yelled and dove into a thicket path that led to a backyard short cut we'd taken for years on our newspaper route. Jerome and Patrick scrambled behind me. We lit over an impossible fence dividing two backyards, skittering across the next street by the orange glow of streetlights, into another dark yard, through the yard and over another tall fence. We covered four or five blocks like this, gliding effortlessly over fences like hurdles. These were high, dividing fences we cleared with an easy spring—I'll never understand how. At last we froze in someone's backyard like three garden gnomes, listening to the faraway shouts from the boys, their bloody promises.

When they faded to quiet, Patrick punched me in the arm and grabbed my shirt.

"You asshole!" he was shaking, wild and bleeding from somewhere. No, I was bleeding. My hand was opened in a long gash, black in the dim moonlight. He was yelling, but not yelling, "You total dick! You could have gotten us killed!"

Finally I wrestled my brother to the dirt, to shut him up. To put his face in the soil for just standing there, doing nothing—

"Boys!" said Jerome, prying us from each other. "Get out of it!"

Maybe it was his accent, or because he called us boys, but we stopped and waited for our referee to call the next play.

"Yes," he said. "Stupid!"

But then he stood up, a four-foot giant, hands punched into his waist. He took a long drink of the cooling night. You could smell the stillness. His eyes glittered over the imaginary expanse, the tepid lay of Lynnwood suburbs. "It is alright with this," he said with a quick nod.

"What are you talking about?!"

"*America.*"

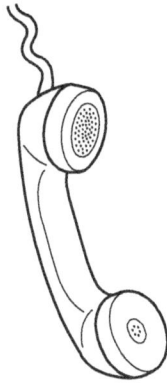

Patrick

Feng Shui

I unlocked my apartment to find my refrigerator had been pulled from its spot and rolled to the middle of the entry. That wasn't the weird thing. The detail that caught my immediate attention was a smear of blood, a blotch indicating a small impact, wiped through with a long trail of finger smears down the side of the appliance.

I dropped the groceries, bracing for an intruder, listening. There was only silence, nobody scrambling out the back door. I shouldered open the door, scalp tingling with alert, and squeezed between the refrigerator and the wall, further into the apartment.

Here was more to this puzzling scene: nothing had been rummaged, or stolen, but everything was rearranged. Chairs had been pulled from the dining table, stacked in the small entry hallway. The couch was pulled from the wall to the middle of the living room. The coffee table was upside down. Someone, or something, had removed the television from its stand and placed it on the carpet, face down. Everything was sprinkled and spritzed with tiny, still-wet droplets of blood.

Further in, the bedrooms revealed more blood. Everywhere I looked I found more. On my pillow and sheets. Seeing the tiny droplets staining the beige hallway carpet, I thought, *there goes the security deposit.*

The only room untouched was the bathroom. It was not clean by any measure because living with my brother meant living with a nightmare bathroom, but at least it was unbloodied. I suppose it was a bonus the tub was in the same place I'd left it that morning.

I looked in on Patrick's room, which was always an assault to the senses. He rigged his stereo to play music on constant, at the highest volumes. The playlist reeled violently between Spiritualized, the Stone Roses, Spacemen 3 and Magnog. This was accompanied by the heavy reek of incense he left on a constant burn.

Today, his room was tossed into a particular disorder. The mattress had been picked up from the floor and was leaning against the wall where it pulled his prized poster of Hope Sandoval from its central placement to a crumple on the ground. His desk was pushed awry from the wall and the shades were bent and twisted askew from the open window—jagged slats of sunlight beamed through the smoky den. Here and there, too, were the telltale globules of blood.

Before he caught me in his room, I shut the bedroom door.

I'd touched nothing, but somehow, I'm certain, he'd sense his sanctuary had been penetrated. The Chi had been sullied and he'd fly off the handle with fiery accusations. No matter. I returned the furniture to its place, cleaning and scrubbing the blood as I went.

I didn't expect an apology for the mess as Patrick was never the apologizing type. But so help me God, by day's end I would have an explanation to what happened in this apartment. I would have the explanation if it meant wringing his goddamn neck with my bare hands.

Since we'd become roommates, the summer slowed to a crawl. I'd just graduated college and was fulfilling an idiotic fantasy to take the summer off. One last hurrah before an inevitable lifetime of work. Taking a summer to do nothing seemed a particularly extravagant bender and its notion, born from privilege and stupidity, seemed irresistible—in theory.

Then there was my brother Patrick, who hated work of any kind. He'd moved in but hadn't bothered to get a job since Mom paid his rent and ensured he was fed. He couldn't have been more thrilled to join in my summer plan and help me burn through a small fortune.

While I was happy for his company I was leary of his mercurial outbursts—per usual of our uneasy bond. As brothers we longed for and were repelled by each other's company. In our inseparable tangle of adoration and loathing, my simple summer plans were somehow turned into a ridiculous and horrible pact: to just let go the oars, so to speak, throw them overboard and see what the summer would bring.

What happened next was a gorgeous and horrible descent to a summer of fever dreams, restless at all hours. Unmoored from the rhythm of regular work, we spent the long, hot days drifting between meals and movies, high or drunk or both. I wish I could say we spent our time more wisely, read more books, or at least exercised. Sometimes we'd go swimming, but that was it for the day.

It was in those empty weeks the distance between us bloomed at an alarming rate.

Patrick had realized his life's calling: the non-committal shuffle between distractions.

He spent an incredible amount of time curating an intricate playlist. He drew doodles, the kind you'd find an idle hand swirling in a dentist's waiting room. He brewed pot after pot of mysterious and putrid teas, which was mostly weeds he'd foraged from the arboretum, or the construction lot next door. He patiently meditated at the guitar on a never-ending exploration of atonal tunings.

I was going nuts.

Doing nothing turned out to be far more difficult than I could've imagined.

With all the freedom to drive anywhere, to do anything, we ended up staying home. This suited Patrick just fine. He'd start a week-long odyssey carving a figurine from a bar of soap while I could find no amount of distraction to quiet the nag that I was becoming more and more useless, marinating in a stagnant privilege that would jelly my spine and I would never be able to work an honest day again. I secretly longed for work, even work I hated and paid shit just for the hope it would balance out the overwhelming feeling I had become a cancer.

So when I got a half-assed part-time job washing dishes at a Thai restaurant, Patrick was immensely hurt. It was an unforgivable betrayal.

His reaction was puzzling since we'd been fighting like cats. I would've thought he'd be elated to have me out of his hair but he said I was a schmuck. I didn't have the imagination to just sit and do nothing.

This had been an underlying theme in our persistent arguments. How he loved to deride my belief in hard work. That I would succumb to a life of work was indicative of my failing to open my eyes to the mysterious "beyond." My inability to look beyond the lies, beyond what we'd been led to believe by those who wanted to enslave us. He always spoke of himself as pitted against a "them," or an elusive "other," in sweeping, dramatic strokes. He argued we were all pathetic consumers, fooled into believing there was a certain way to live your life, and living your life within those constraints was the surest sign of idiocy. He compared this to the *Matrix*, a movie he referenced often, to describe the nebulous prison in which we were trapped.

This was all heady, exhausting stuff that, somehow, precluded him from contributing to the water or electric bills. This was compounded by our mutual inability and disinterest in fighting with any degree of civility. Though soaring and profound, our arguments rarely left anything besides scorched earth.

I finally sat down to look around my re-rearranged living room. How much blood had I cleaned? How much had I overlooked?

I was speculating on this when the front door swung open, and Patrick came bouldering in, clutching his cat like a football.

Louie the cat leapt from his grasp and perched in my lap. He settled in a warm curl, motoring hard.

In the kitchen, Patrick turned on a burner and rummaged around the cabinet he'd commandeered for his tea.

"What's new?" I asked, casually.

Patrick said nothing. He slammed the cabinet and slammed the kettle on the burner. The cat sprung from my lap. I made my way to the kitchen where Patrick was watching the kettle.

"I rearranged the apartment," I said.

He didn't look up. I pressed further into the kitchen, pushing against the opposing force field radiating between us. His knuckles were white.

"It's a lot like it was before but, you know, without all the blood—"

"What!?" he hissed. "What do you want from me?"

"What do I want?" I said, cool but shaky. "I want to know what fucking happened in our fucking apartment."

"Louie caught a bird."

I waited for more.

"And?"

"*And*, it wasn't dead. 'the fuck do you think happened?"

I told him what I thought happened. That maybe someone had been murdered and their body swung around the apartment. But Patrick was done explaining. It would appear I'd have to piece together the rest on my own. Really, I had all the details I needed: Louie caught the bird and brought it in through the bedroom window Patrick refused to close (even in a mid-winter snap, heaters on roar, he left the window open for the breeze). Unkilled and bleeding, the bird, something large probably, took flight with Patrick chasing it behind appliances, under furniture, frantic in the creature's sputtering throes.

Characteristic to all of my brother's incredible explanations was the dearth of answers. In their stead, the implied host of infuriating questions.

What is the big deal?

What else should he have done? Let the bird fly around and die on its own?

Why would he have cleaned the apartment? If he had to hurry the dead bird to the vet, with the cat, in the same carrier?

Why didn't I just—let it go?

That's what he wanted to know, why I wouldn't just drop it. He was genuinely bewildered and red-faced and furious I could be so upset when it was he, whose mellow had been harshed. His perfect day that'd been ruined.

"Just because you beat me to putting away the furniture—"

"And cleaning the blood."

"*And* cleaning the blood. Doesn't mean I wasn't going to clean up. So don't think you get to lord this over me, like you do with everything else!"

He took that and pushed past the trap I'd made of our kitchen. Patrick simply wasn't interested in discussing this any longer. He wasn't interested in even being part of this scene, until the topic du jour had passed beyond an unspoken statute of limitations, sometimes only a day or two, until its rehashing was more an offense than the topic it addressed.

Something had snapped, just then, and I didn't chase after

him like I usually did.

Usually, I'd hold him at the shoulders and wrestle him to the ground, in spite of his slashing fingernails (he had no reservations about a dirty fight). That may have worked once, long ago, shocking him to a place he could be reached. But he'd quickly developed a tolerance for even that. He'd let me hold him down, face blank, hearing nothing. I didn't pursue him then because this was the moment I realized, at last, he'd slipped into a realm I was not allowed. To follow him there would be a violation.

This was the moment I officially let go of my brother.

To cut him loose was, of course, the bitter betrayal. But I did it anyway.

It was just the way it was.

He slammed the door to his room. The discussion was over.

The Spacemen 3's "The Perfect Prescription" blasted behind his door as choking incense filled the apartment. I stayed in the kitchen, crippled by the loss, the devastating departure of my beautiful brother. The beautiful boy!

The kettle rang out a furious boil. I turned off the burner and set the kettle aside. He was not coming out for tea. It was likely he wouldn't come out of his room for days, but the hot water was there, for when he was ready.

Time and the Passing of Time

When my wife finally came home, I told her we were getting a divorce and I was late for work. If she'd have come home earlier, there would've been more time to talk things over. As it was, she'd been out all night, who knows where.

Secretly, I was grateful to slip away since, really, there was nothing to discuss, right away at least. We could negotiate the nuts and bolts of our separation later. The first thing we needed was time for reflection and grief, a great regrouping we would need to learn alone.

"How did you know?" she asked, curious but indifferent, perched halfway up the stairs and wrapped in that ridiculous red dress.

"Are you kidding?" I said, gathering my coat. "A husband knows. I even know it's someone you work with."

The way she fell apart indicated my wild guess was right on the mark. For the briefest moment, I thought her racking sobs were for me, until she surprised me with a request.

"Please!" she called out. "Please don't tell anyone at work!"

"What?!"

"You're not going to tell. Are you?"

I don't think she was trying to be intentionally cruel (our marriage had certainly been plagued by unhinged cruelty), rather, her request smacked closer to the tone-deaf horribleness that had become commonplace between us. I didn't point out how depressing this was, that her only concern was for job security, what coworkers would think of her affair. The dissolution of her marriage didn't even seem to register.

I was going to point out how this was a downright rotten way to be, but caught myself before saying anything. She'd only be confused as to why this was problematic and I didn't have the stomach for that kind of blow.

Thankfully, I said nothing.

I shut the front door and walked to my car.

It had been a wet and warm July in the Pacific Northwest. It was not yet seven in the morning and a thick, downy mist blanketed the lawns and fences and rooftops. The day was young and uncertain when I got in the car and drove through the great Skagit Valley into the worst day of my life.

During the half hour drive to work, I decided to get back in touch with my family. This was quite a thing since we'd not spoken in years. At last, the constant triage of my floundering marriage had come to its horrible conclusion and I was finally free to reconnect with them. I missed them terribly and decided to call on my lunch break. We would have a good talk and maybe even after work I would drive south to see them, shake their hands and catch up. Of course, *if*—if they would even speak to me again.

There were many reasons for removing myself from my family, none of which were worth recounting. Time, and the passing of time, had seen to that. If they asked for an explanation, I'd stick to what I knew: we were due for a great recalibration, a redrawing of boundaries. That would be a hard sell after the years we'd spent apart. My brother and sisters and parents, our great sprawling matriarchy of cousins and aunts, all had plenty of time to stew in their own conclusions. Likely they'd think I just wanted to lash out and hurt people, or my mind had been twisted by a wicked therapist or I'd simply gone crazy.

Maybe they'd even suspect I was finally broke and returning to the family for money. There was the looming divorce, that too would provide a wealth of speculation. Regardless of what anyone may have concluded, or would suspect, we'd give it a try anyway.

Maybe we could start over?

Maybe everything was ruined?

I would find out on my lunch break.

When I arrived at work, the Bee family was at it again. They were all standing in line for their daily scam.

I called them the Bee family because of their ravenous appetite for sugary 24-ounce milkshakes. The mother and her three creepy, bee larvae children came in once a day to suck down their beverages with an insect intensity.

Their scam began the previous summer when one of these humongous beverages was dropped on the ground. When I came around with a mop, one of the girls was sobbing at the giant mess. I tried to console her and tell her it would be okay until I realized her worsening hysteria wasn't for the mess on the ground, but rather for the half of her drink she wouldn't get to finish. Her sisters even taunted her with their drinks, sucking slowly from their straws and pushing her to an insane rage.

The situation was diffused by simply remaking the child's drink. But this led to a trickier injustice: the other children complained even louder, both wailing and sobbing, because their sister was going to get more than they did, a shake and a half, which wasn't fair.

Soon as the remade drink was set on the bar, a little pair of sticky hands shot up from below the counter and the drink disappeared. The girl pounced on the straw and her sisters dissolved into tears.

"Now look what I have to deal with!" their mother scorned.

"Thanks. *Thanks a lot!*"

The next day the Bees returned, and ordered the same beverages. The kids drank half and then accidentally threw all three of their drinks on the floor and demanded another, which we obliged. This became a frequent routine. Even their mother occasionally threw her beverage on the ground.

One day I caught them in the act. I'd been following them, pretending to dust a shelf nearby. The girls drank almost all their shake, looked left and then right and chucked the almost empty cup on the floor. There were tears and screaming.

Again, their mother happily suggested we remake the ruined beverages.

That was the day I declined her offer. I assured her we could not possibly accommodate them anymore. She, of course, lost her shit. She raised all sorts of holy hell in our cafe, screaming and throwing things. Later that day a district-wide email was sent out, renewing our "Just Say Yes" policy. The situation I'd caused was called out and it was passively determined "those involved" had run afoul of our official corporate policy on freebie scams. So it was decided, we would honor our fantastic obligation to the Bee family who happily accepted our apology and resumed their incredible diet with aplomb.

Who could blame them?

But that morning was different. Something had shifted during my commute to work and I'd become oddly bloodthirsty. I wasn't going to mop up their shit anymore. District policy be damned, I wasn't going to stand for this. Starting right then and there, I wasn't going to take shit from anyone. Not anymore.

I met the Bee mother in line and told her to get out of our cafe. I told them they could never come back. Of course she was livid and protested, but I walked her and her insect children backwards, out of the cafe. They could raise all their fuss outside in the parking lot.

My decision shocked the cafe silent, except for Sheryl Crow's "Everyday is a Winding Road" on the radio. There was no applause, or cheers. In fact, everyone was furious with me. The same employees who hated the Bee family and endlessly complained of their scam and their behavior, many who even called it child abuse, were mysteriously irate at my sudden decision. They wasted no time voicing their disapproval and almost rejoiced at the prospect of my termination.

I didn't care about any of that. Not anymore. I put on my apron, cleaned up the displays the Bee family tossed on their way out. Before I could begin my shift in earnest, the store manager pulled me aside.

"Maybe we should sit down for a moment, check in?"

We took a seat in the cafe. Erica was my manager, but also a friend of mine, and I told her about my morning. When I told her about the divorce, she only said, "Yeah."

"You don't sound surprised," I said.

"No! I mean, it's awful but it's probably for the best. How are you?"

"I feel great!" I lied. "Like a new man! And I'm not going to take any of this shit anymore."

"Good luck with that one," she laughed. "Does this mean I can finally call your wife a bitch? Because she's a—"

"No."

Erica huffed, "Spoilsport."

Erica tore up my corrective action paperwork. Considering the circumstances, she was going to give me a pass. Secretly, she was elated someone finally put the Bee family in their place and was probably relieved it didn't have to be her.

A barista leaned over the counter, her palm on the phone, "Phone call for you, Nate."

"I'm not taking it."

"I can take it if you like," offered Erica.

"Absolutely not," I said. "Please take a message—"

"It's urgent," she pressed.

"It's not urgent."

"Tell his wife," said Erica, "She'll just have to wait."

"It's not his wife," she said. "It's his sister."

The coincidence was uncanny.

I have to say, I was impressed they'd found me. Nobody in my family knew where I worked. They had no forwarding address or phone number. The legwork that must have gone into locating that phone number was incredible.

The barista held out the phone, head cocked and hand on her hip. She was still fuming I hadn't been fired over the recent scene. I took the phone and said, "Thank you."

"Whatever."

I held out the phone: family.

"Hello?"

"Don't hang up!" said my sister.

"How did you get this number?"

"Patrick is dead."

I sat down.

"Did you hear me? He's dead and you need to come home."

"I heard you," I said dumbly.

I remember almost none of our conversation. I remember it was delicate and clumsy and bound inexorably with resentment and anger and overwhelming grief. It was short. When I hung up the phone, Erica, who'd been eavesdropping nearby cut me off.

She held up her hands, "Go."

This next part is also fuzzy, and I'm still grasping at the facts.

I don't remember the short walk to my car. I remember noticing my hands were on the steering wheel, but how long had I been sitting there, in the parking lot? I started driving, but I don't remember if I drove north, to my house, or if I drove straightaway south, for my parents' house. It seems a large detail to overlook.

I probably shouldn't have been driving at all. Traffic was suddenly arbitrary and foreign, all cars coming at me. I felt like I was operating my car from a faraway distance, like a passenger in the back seat, calling out the commands to the body up front—"A little more gas, now brake. Left turn signal, clutch then second gear…"

Just that morning I'd obsessively orchestrated a family reunion. Hoping for a graceful reintroduction, I'd recounted the details, predicted maneuvers around triggers and trap doors. I'd attempted to unravel the great juggernaut of guilt and satisfaction in our discommunication, to chart some kind of a way forward. All that was gone now.

Now there was simply no more time. There was only a great urgency—stumbling forward and grasping, we would be thrown together and attempt to reacquaint ourselves. I would reintroduce myself to my sisters and mom and dad. I had a new brother in-law, and some nieces and nephews I was looking forward to meeting as well.

When I arrived at the great house of my childhood, I swam to the front door.

I had been away so long, to just let myself in seemed presumptuous. I knocked instead and waited, noting the sign above the doorbell: "No Solicitors." Alissa's two boys opened the door and surprised me by rushing out, clinging to my pants and shouting, "It's Uncle Patrick! We found Uncle Patrick!"

I hugged them back, desperately.

"Nope," I said. "I'm just Nate. Patrick and I look a lot alike."

The Prank

Our Greyhound bus rumbled away from the Portland terminal with Patrick and me running after it, screaming and trying to flag it down. The bus quickly accelerated beyond reach until it slowed for a red light down the street, then ground to a halt. I doubled in, running past my legs, churning arms, through a parking lot, across a busy street and down the next block to the bus, idling cooly at the red light.

I was going to catch it!

I was just a couple car lengths away now. Surely the driver could see the two small boys he'd picked up in Seattle panicking in his rear view mirror. The light turned green and the muddy bus jumped forward with a hiss. I caught hold of the bumper, whacking the side of the bus as it kicked into gear and slipped away.

We chased it up the Broadway Bridge until it was gone, taking all our bags and tickets and everything we brought for a week of camping in Yosemite with it. We collapsed for breath, hands on our knees, not far from the yawning mouth of the bascule bridge.

The city and its skyline suddenly seemed different from the cozy town, like a toy Seattle, we'd admired on the bus ride in. Maybe it was because we just lost everything, but the city now appeared slanted and cruel, but also focused and beautiful. From the bridge we could see the gnarly east riverbank, the thick, grey downtown all the way up to the towering west hills—steaming thick curtains of morning fog—glowing in the rising sun. The greasy river below was glassy slick, swirling milky blue.

"HelloooOOoo?" my brother was yelling. "Are you even listening to me?"

He'd not been swept up by the view as I had.

"What are we going to do now?!"

I shot back, "You were the one who insisted on playing another video game!"

"That's not true!" he shouted.

Yes it was. We only had a half hour layover in Portland— just enough time to stretch our legs, and Patrick had thrown himself to the terminal arcade with a stubborn magnetism. It was my job to keep track of my impossible brother, at least until I could pawn him off on our older sister we were meeting in Yosemite.

Rather than stand guard like an idiot, I joined him in a couple video games and immediately lost track of time. The very moment I remembered where we were, why we were there, I looked out the window to the sickly specter of our bus pulling away.

From the bridge, we ran back to the station to an oddly pissed-off woman at the ticketing window. She slapped her way through a magazine as I unrolled our stupid story. When I was finished, she simply shrugged, almost relishing how little there was to be done. She offered only one certainty: there was no way to get ahold of the driver, and in all likelihood our bags and tickets and everything was probably already stolen by someone on the bus.

"You know," I told her. "You're not very helpful."

She shrugged again, back to her magazine, "Cruel to be kind."

Patrick was fidgeting on the bench where I'd commanded him to stay put.

"So?" he asked.

"So, we have to call home," I said.

"Fuck that!" he said, hands up. "No way."

"You have a better idea?"

"Yeah. *Not* calling home!"

"And do what?"

"We can hitchhike. Unless you're too scared?"

"Yeah," I said. "Because we're pros at hitching rides, and then what? Tell our driver to chase down our bus? Don't be an asshole!'"

"Fine," said my asshole brother. "Call home. See if I care."

Mom picked up the line, instantly suspicious. When I told her what happened, she descended into hysterics.

"I put you on the bus myself!" she screamed. "All you had to do was stay—*on the bus*. How could you—"

There was a struggle on the other end and Alissa, my oldest sister, took the line. Alissa stepped in whenever she thought Mom was about to be too lenient with us, which was always.

She led with a feigned calm, wanting to know what we expected.

"What do you expect?" she said. "You always do this. You waste your time and your money on your stupid video games and this is what happens. Honestly, I don't know what you called here for."

"We're stranded," I reminded her. "In Portland."

"Tough shit," she said and hung up the phone.

Dizzy with panic, I returned to the bench where I'd left Patrick. He was gone. I'd managed to get us perfectly stranded in a strange city and just as easily, misplaced my twelve-year-old brother.

I finally found him trying to hang out with the homeless crowd, camped at the far end of the bus station. A man with no shoes watched me tentatively approaching. He said, "Whoa! You guys must be brothers!" His feet were cracked and bleeding. He patted Patrick on the back, "This little guy's a trip! Cool dude. Yeah—"

"We need to go," I said.

"Where?" said Patrick, the man's hand still on his back.

"How did your phone call go?"

"We're screwed."

"*You're* screwed," he said. He coolly pushed a bummed cigarette behind his ear. "I'm doing fine."

"Yeah dude," said another man who was crawling with ferrets. "Your brother's cool, he'll be fine here, with us."

Patrick crossed his arms defiantly. He looked downright ridiculous with this crowd: a pudgy simpleton from the suburbs, flirting with desperate, lecherous men with hands like broken cement and only a handful of teeth scattered among them. They reeked of a urine brine and the sweet-sour wheeze of malt liquor.

"We need to go," I said, grabbing his arm. "*Now!*"

"Fuck you!" Patrick shrieked, scratching me with his fingernails.

The man with the ferrets jumped to his feet. He put his hand on my chest.

"Didn't you hear him?" he said, licking his chapped, white lips. He gave me a little push. "Leave him alone."

A man in a Greyhound uniform stepped in. He said, "Nate Barber? Patrick Barber? We've got a bus for you, it's leaving right now."

I didn't ask how he knew our names. I didn't ask Patrick if he was ready to leave his new friends. Instead, I snatched my brother by each wrist and drug him mercilessly, kicking and screaming across the terminal after this Greyhound saint who was almost running to the departures garage. He shouted into his walkie-talkie, "Hold the door! I found them. We're almost there!"

He looked back to make sure we were still following and was horrified by what he saw.

Patrick always threw the most impressive tantrums. Since he couldn't shake loose of my grip, he simply stopped walking and collapsed to the ground, hollering like he was being peeled alive. I clung after the station porter like he was a lifeline. To keep up, I simply dragged my brother on the ground behind me.

Our bus was nearly full, idling. The driver drummed the steering wheel impatiently. The passengers pressed to the windows, watching this godforsaken mess approach their bus, then realizing they'd be sharing their long, claustrophobic ride with these two boys: Patrick, who seemed to be suffering a seizure, and myself, who seemed intent on kicking his ass inside out.

The station agent stepped aside, nodding to the grumpy driver, and I threw Patrick into the bus as you would throw a wad of knotted, uncooperative laundry into a dryer.

How had we gotten on this bus? How were we magically returned to our original route? It was a fantastic mystery until our quick layover in Sacramento. Another Greyhound agent was waiting for us, holding our bags. He looked grey and exhausted.

"You must be the Barber boys?" he said, holding out our luggage. "Your sister's wicked with a telephone. She's had all of us here, on the phone. It's because of her—well, you should give her a call and a thank-you."

With that, he took a deep breath, ceremoniously held out our bags and dropped them with such relief I had to wonder, *what had Alissa done to this poor man?*

How she was able to squeeze competency, compassion even, from the stubbornly cynical and indifferent Greyhound clerks was another mystery. But there we were, on the last leg of our trip to Yosemite, with our bags and all of our ten fingers and toes.

"Everything is still here!" I rejoiced, rooting through my bag. "Nothing is missing!"

Patrick shrugged, "Whoop-de-doo." He gathered his duffle, hoisting it dramatically as if he'd just been reunited with an albatross. Secretly, he was beside himself to see his bag again, his Walkman and all his tapes, his collection of chapsticks and fourteen pairs of socks, but he didn't dare to show a whiff of relief as it would acknowledge the great debt we now owed our capable sister.

I wasn't excited either, to become the steward of a favor I could never repay, and would probably be reminded of often, but there was no mistaking: we owed her, big time.

Patrick chafed instantly at this powerful shift in familial dynamics and concluded, as only my brother could, he'd somehow been tricked. He dismissed the entire episode as some immeasurably complex plot to allow our sister the upper hand.

We resumed our seats, secluded to opposite ends of the bus, in part due to necessity, since the bus was packed when we boarded, but also because one of us surely would have strangled the other had we been seated together.

The driver made his last call and shut the doors.

There was a commotion at the front of the bus. I looked, everyone looked, to see what was all the fuss. There was Patrick haranguing the driver to let him off the bus. He had to pee. I watched in horror as he just stood up and marched right out the doors, across the terminal, inside the station. And then I noticed everyone was looking at me, bewildered and waiting for an explanation.

I offered, feebly, "He's got a thing for clean bathrooms."

One of the many things I admired about my brother was his complete disregard for anything that didn't suit him. His total indifference and audacity was a spectacle to behold.

Anyone else would have used the rank little shithole in the back of the bus. If that was not possible, anyone else would have either held it in, or ran like hell, apologizing profusely to the bus full of people whose already lengthy journey was being further delayed by a fickle bladder and a refusal to negotiate a bus toilet. Anyone else would have been speedy about their business, instead of reading through an entire *People* magazine, which is how long Patrick was in there before he finally sauntered out, whistling-skippy, just strolling along with his hands in his pockets.

All eyes on that bus licked me up and down. My ears burned and I crumpled in with embarrassment.

Not just this once, the great shame he could not register fell heavy on me. I'd been gifted with the ability to sponge in discomfort, to writhe in its spotlight, and it made me furiously jealous of him. I longed to cut a similarly carefree swath as Patrick was so effortlessly capable. I have tried to emulate his fearlessness, but I could never duplicate his jut chin and boyish dismissal, signaling to everyone on this murder bus they could all, collectively, go and fuck themselves.

Gwyneth made the hour drive from Yosemite Village to meet us at our stop, which was nothing more than a shot-up and rusted sign pinned to the desolate shoulder of a rural California highway. She arrived to find just that, and no brothers. She drove twenty minutes to the nearest gas station to call home, and Alissa and Mom gave her an earful. Our arrival was delayed six hours—just enough time to make waiting around unbearable.

By the time we finally arrived, Gwyneth was happy to see us but already exhausted by her charge as our surrogate care-taker. Her time in the national park had been good to her, good enough that she forgot how much a pain in the ass her family could be. The reminder came with a swift sting, the grim prospect of spending the next week guiding us through Yosemite, then driving us north, home.

Patrick, still on the defensive, wedged himself in the back seat of our sister's Volkswagen Rabbit with his headphones.

"Nice to see you too," Gwyneth offered. But Patrick's eyes were already closed, earphones squealing.

"We're not talking," I said. "Not since Portland—"

"Alissa already told me."

"*Her* side of the story," I said.

"You've got a better version?!"

We said nothing, heading into Yosemite Valley.

We followed the 120, a spare, lulling two-lane road that swayed through dry pines. This was forest, but foreign and weird, absent the lush underbrush of our northwest forests. The ground was a pack of dry needles and wisps of fragrant brush, the smell of sap and dirty sage in the chapped summer air. When the road opened to the great shouldered crags of the rocky valley, Patrick took off his headphones and rolled down the window. The car filled with the cool air, heavy with the mineral mist from the grinding Merced River. The water was blue grey in calm pools and deep green eddies, split by sudden, churning rapids.

"Have you gone swimming in that?!" said Patrick, eagerly thumping the back of Gwyneth's seat.

Gwyneth said, "Only because I was drunk. It's cold as hell."

"Pull over!" he insisted, already unbuckling his seatbelt.

She pulled the car to the shoulder, Patrick and I stripped to our underwear and threw ourselves into the river and, just as quickly, scrambled back to shore. The sight of us, frozen and purple lips and chattering teeth in our sagging briefs had Gwyneth doubled over the hood of the Rabbit. She couldn't help herself, she just laughed and laughed, until we were laughing too. I couldn't say what was so funny, but by the time we rolled into Yosemite Village, we were all peeling with hysterics like a car full of lunatics ready to strike terror in the hearts of the tourists and day hikers.

Gwyneth and Patrick tucked into the trails with a calm sprint. They knowingly hooked their thumbs to the wide shoulder straps of their huge packs and sailed up switchbacks with a ruthless ease.

Much of what I recall of those spectacular trails was my hurrying feet, tripping to catch up. My legs were drained and shaky. I cursed my short limbs. Until then my short legs had only presented the minor inconvenience of hemming every pair of pants. But the practical advantage of long, graceful legs had never been fully impressed until seeing my brother and sister stilt-gliding through an alpine meadow like a pair of giraffes.

Here and there they stopped to wait for me, but by the time I limped to their spot they were fully rested, already gathering their bags.

"You're doing great!" Patrick encouraged.

"Fuck—" I gasped. "Off."

"Look up!" Gwyneth suggested. "Don't forget to look up!"

And off they went, playfully scrambling up a shale slide.

She was right, I was missing the view with my head-down, full-on charge after them.

When I did look up there was a stunning postcard vista, immeasurable and humbling. A feast for a view! But when I looked to my siblings to share the moment, they were gone, far up the trail again.

The valley was dry as a matchbox. Patrick and I had planned to disregard the burn ban, which extended to camp-fires. Patrick even surrendered a valuable portion of his back-pack to a jumbo bag of marshmallows.

What was camping without a campfire?

We were nonplussed to discover Gwyneth was a stickler for the park's rules. She was steadfast in her enforcement of this and many other restrictions. After all, she'd just spent a year witnessing waves of tourists wreak havoc with the modest guidelines set by the national park's sensible stewards.

At the day's end, we sat in the dark, listening to Gwyneth regale the year of atrocities committed by the plagues of sun-burned tourists, cranky and entitled, who romped, willy-nilly,

off the trail boundaries and scratched their initials into anything but solid granite. They started fires like deranged pyro-
maniacs and left piles of beer cans and styrofoam nests wherever they pleased.

Patrick cooked some marshmallows with a lighter. Then
we just ate plain, cold marshmallows. To Gwyneth's and my
great relief, Patrick was surprisingly good humored, even when
the park's cruel terrain boiled us down to the hungry essentials
of food and water and time. His notorious hassle about bowel
movements, his finicky demand for pristine restrooms, went
completely unmentioned. When faced with the harsh reality of
the "pack-it-in, pack-it-out" rule of hikers' etiquette, he didn't
utter a single complaint, and we were allowed to enjoy our hike,
happily shitting into plastic bags which we carried out of the
park with us.

When we emerged from the backcountry, limping and chis-
eled and crazy, we were surprised (and not surprised) to find
ourselves caught in a bond that hadn't been there before.
Somewhere in there, we'd managed to shake out the native language that eluded our childhood and we reveled in its common
perspective: a raunchy series of inside jokes and grumbling cyn-
icism about the banal world awaiting us.

We took nothing from Yosemite, aside from what we'd
found: a fleeting glimpse at camaraderie, powerful enough to
inspire a horrible and fantastic prank, one last hurrah to return
us home. Mom and Alissa had no idea of the terrible meteor
hurtling homeward.

We let Patrick out at the top of our cul-de-sac with his backpack.

Gwyneth and I drove back to the 7-Eleven, allowing Patrick enough time to sneak his way home before we called. I held the receiver so we could both hear the phone ring.

Mom answered, "Hello?"

"Hi," I said. "It's me."

"How's your trip?" she said, tentatively. "Are you almost home?"

"Yeah, there's a bit of a problem."

"A problem?"

"We had a fight."

"Who?!"

"Patrick. He just left, said he was going to hitchhike home."

"What?!"

"We told him not to leave but he just—left."

There was a struggle on the other line.

Alissa took the line, "What's going on? What problem?"

For my older sister, I recounted our rehearsed story in my favorite deadpan. I told her about how we'd gotten into another fight at the Oregon sand dunes the day before and we hadn't seen Patrick since. Gwyneth was holding her mouth, trying not to make any noise. This played right into our older sister's suspicions that we were all highly irresponsible and left a wake of enormous catastrophes that were somehow her responsibility to mop up.

"Yesterday?" she asked.

"I know, right?"

"And you're just calling? Just now?!"

"Well, I figure it's a thing now. Since he's like, missing and all."

"Put your sister on the phone."

I said, "Sure thing!"

I palmed the phone and we both fell apart. Oh, it was hilarious! Gwyneth finally wiped away tears, straightened up and took the line.

"Hey, yeah," she said in her best hippy voice. "You heard about Pat—"

There was quite a din from the other line. Gwyneth's face drained. She nodded, soaking up an earful. Looking at the ground, saying, "No, but—" and "Yeah, but—" There was nowhere to toe-in and bring the joke around. It was slipping away, unraveling into madness.

There was a pause and Gwyneth put her palm against the phone, "They just heard the doorbell."

"It took him long enough!" I said.

She held out the phone and we both listened in to the tiny pandemonium erupting from the ear piece. There sure was a lot of shouting. Alissa and mom were shouting at Patrick. Patrick was shouting back. Duffy, our dog, joined the awful chorus, howling like crazy.

Sickened, Gwyneth hung up the phone.

We took our time getting back in the car, not wanting to drive home. We were in deep trouble, that much was certain. Somewhere out there, Patrick was getting his bones picked clean and for that, we were truly sorry. But with the windows down, and such a nice summer day, Gwyneth drove right past our cul-de-sac, tacking one more mile to our trip.

Maybe she didn't. I like to think she did.

Anyway, it was so long ago.

About the author

Keep an eye out for Nathaniel Barber's forthcoming works: a second collection of non-fiction shorts (with a good helping of fiction thrown in for good measure) and two collections of poetry—grown up poems for children and childish poems for grown ups. All works written and edited almost exclusively between the hours of 3:00-6:00 AM from his kitchen table. Currently, Mr. Barber lives in Portland, Oregon with his wife and daughter and a cat.